MICKEY ROURKE

Published by Transit Publishing Inc.

ISBN: 978-1-926745-40-4

Cover design: François Turgeon
Text design and composition: Nassim Bahloul

Cover photo:
© Steve Read/Contour Getty Images

Transit Publishing Inc.
1996 St-Joseph Boulevard East
Montreal, QC
H2H 1E3

Tel: 514-273-0123
www.transitpublishing.com

Printed and Bound in Canada

Sandro Monetti

MICKEY ROURKE:
WRESTLING WITH DEMONS

CONTENTS

PREFACE

"Most people are never lucky enough to hang out with their heroes, but tonight I'm so fortunate to share the stage with someone who has greatly inspired and entertained me for years. Ladies and gentlemen... Mickey Rourke!"

With those words, I introduced the comeback king of Hollywood at a Q&A following the British Academy screening in Los Angeles of his life-changing movie *The Wrestler*. The large crowd got to its feet, clapping and cheering, giving an almost deafening ovation to show huge appreciation and sweet affection for a star who was finally receiving the recognition his immense talent deserved.

Every year, during what Hollywood calls "awards season," I interview the big movie stars in the running for the film industry's glittering prizes at special screenings held for the various groups who vote for these awards. The likes of Helen Mirren, Cate Blanchett, Javier Bardem, and Viggo Mortensen would take their turns talking to me and the audience about their prestigious projects. But it always seemed as if someone was missing from this annual glory circuit, and that was the most utterly mesmerizing and intriguing actor of his generation.

When Mickey Rourke burst onto the scene over twenty-five years ago, he made an instant impact in movies like *9½ Weeks* and *Rumble Fish*, and he was widely hailed as the most exciting new acting talent since James Dean or Marlon Brando. Fans like me certainly thought so and expected a string of Oscars, BAFTAs and blockbusters to follow. But a self-destructive tendency of almost Shakespearian proportion meant it didn't work out that way.

A succession of disastrous choices derailed his Hollywood career. His reputation for fighting with producers, showing up late to sets, not sticking to the script, bad-mouthing colleagues, and raising hell wherever he went served to burn all his bridges in Tinseltown. He looked washed-up, a has-been who would never return to the big time.

Mickey then made the extraordinary decision to change careers and become a professional boxer. He won his fights but lost his Hollywood looks, with the features that made him famous battered to a pulp. Some freaky facial surgery didn't help. After retiring from the ring, a need for cash motivated his return to acting, but a succession of dud films looked to have finished him off for good. He had two broken marriages behind him, lost his brother to cancer, was all alone in the world, and had nothing going for him except his enduring talent.

But there's still magic in the Hollywood hills and sometimes it only takes one or two great performances to turn an actor's fortunes around and put him back on top. First came his stunning supporting role as tough but tender vigilante Marv in 2005's *Sin City*. Then, late in 2008, the buzz about Mickey's lead performance in a low-budget but high-quality new movie entitled *The Wrestler* – sparked by glowing reviews and film festival prizes – rapidly grew into a crescendo that screamed from the rooftops one loud and clear message: "Mickey is back!"

The title character he played, Randy "The Ram" Robinson, a once-great wrestler now seemingly past his prime and beaten down by life but looking for a return to the big time, had so many parallels with Mickey's own roller-coaster life that it was hard to see where the character began and the man playing him ended.

The critics raved about his career-reviving performance and as he did the rounds of press conferences, Q&As, and personal appearances to promote the movie, Mickey not only found himself in the running for Best Actor Oscar but also realized there had been a silent army of Mickey Rourke fans out there who were now emerging from the shadows to shake his hand and share their enthusiasm for his current success.

I was one of them. As an international showbiz reporter for Britain's biggest newspapers, I have covered Mickey's headline-hitting career for two decades, attending his countless entertaining press conferences around the globe. As a fan, I bought tickets to his fights, became a frequent customer at the tiny café he used to own, and eagerly went to see every single one of his films, even those most people have never heard of – like *Picture Claire, Fall Time,* and the killer insect movie *They Crawl.*

For those of us who had followed his career so closely, it was a great thrill when *The Wrestler* saw this dazzling and charismatic performer rebound from the wilderness to the big time.

And so it was that, as one of the actors in contention for honors, he set foot on the awards circuit and our paths crossed, for the first time in years, at that British Academy of Film and Television Arts LA screening of *The Wrestler.* Mickey didn't disappoint. He was everything I expected – tall and solid, moving with a tough guy swagger, shaking hands with sausage-like fingers, and showing up with a little dog and a large entourage. The dog was Loki, a seventeen-year-old Chihuahua that had become his constant companion, and the lively entourage included action star Jason Statham, model Lisa Snowdon, and wrestling legend Rowdy Roddy Piper. Mickey was flamboyantly dressed, as usual, and I was, too, which prompted my hero to greet me with the words, "Have you been raiding my closet?"

Fascinated to see the once down-and-out actor who had suddenly become Hollywood's darling again, the packed crowd hung on his every word as Mickey related his comeback tale to me on stage, then graciously answered all the audience questions and seemingly shook every hand. The event ran way over time, but not a single person left before the end.

Off stage, Mickey and I talked more about how far he'd come and what an extraordinary life he'd had. It's been quite a journey, and I hope you'll enjoy reading about it over the course of the following chapters.

Mickey Rourke: Wrestling with Demons uncovers many fresh and fascinating stories about one of the most colorful figures in film history. From the night he set his home on fire to the day he trembled while having his ear pierced, it's all here, along with behind-the-scenes revelations from his films, including the movie he made in return for a paper bag stuffed with cash and the film for which he got into character by boarding a plane dressed as a woman.

Written with affection and insight but at the same time

pulling no punches, this book aims to be a worthy tribute to, and an entertaining document of, a turbulent life lived from one huge drama to another by a bewitching actor who is as talented as he is troubled.

Mickey, thanks for the memories and all the great moments still to come.

Sandro Monetti
Beverly Hills, California, Summer 2010

1
The Nightmare Years

Desperate, broken down, and battered by setbacks, Mickey Rourke slumped to his knees in a New York church and prayed to a wooden sculpture of St Jude for the strength to stop himself doing what he was about to do.

He had come to 42nd Street's Church of the Holy Cross one damp, dreadful day in the mid-1990s feeling at his lowest ebb and looking for guidance from, appropriately, the patron saint of lost causes. Now, with his acting career all washed up, his money gone, and his wife, Carré Otis, walking out on him, Mickey was tormented by both suicidal and murderous thoughts.

He had a pistol in his pocket and a revenge plan in mind to do some serious harm to a man he says attacked his estranged wife. And, after that, he'd maybe turn the gun on himself.

The pain in his head felt unbearable as he reflected on the mess his life had become and how he had driven away the beautiful woman he loved so much. From his other pocket Mickey took a handwritten letter of apology he had written to Carré. Reading the sad note over and over again, he wondered if these would be the last words he would ever write.

Then he suddenly felt a reassuring hand on his shoulder. He turned and looked into the kindly eyes of the parish priest. Father Peter Colapietro was used to seeing despairing down-

and-outs show up at the rundown, red-brick church. On this occasion, though, he immediately recognized this tormented soul as the fallen movie star who a decade earlier had been one of Hollywood's biggest names, thanks to films like *9½ Weeks*, *Rumble Fish*, and one that the priest had seen fifteen times, *Angel Heart*.

Father Peter had Mickey tell him his troubles and then got him to hand over the gun after asking: "Where in the Bible does it say, 'Vengeance is mine, says Mickey Rourke?'" They lit a candle together and the priest assured the actor, long a man of faith, that God would give him the strength he needed. Father Peter watched Mickey fold and carefully place the note to Carré behind St. Jude's statue and then led him to the rectory where he started a conversation with the desolate star, gently asking what had led him to such a dark place in his life.

It was a story that started only a few miles away across New York, but left a legacy of pain that has stayed with Mickey forever.

* * *

Mickey Rourke has not had a birthday party since he was six. That was the year his parents split up, and he has not felt like celebrating since then. He has described his upbringing as "unusual, crazy and violent" and says if he had the choice of living his childhood all over again, he would rather not have been born.

Life was a struggle from the start for Philip Andre Rourke

Jr. who, just like his character in *The Wrestler*, Robin Robinson, avoids using his given name. He came to be known as Mickey due to a combination of his family's Irish ancestry (the ancestors came from Cork) and his father being a huge fan of baseball star Mickey Mantle.

Mickey Rourke was born in Schenectady, New York, on 16 September 1956 according to his official biography, although other sources, including police arrest records and school files in Miami, state he entered the world in 1952. Many actors shave a few years off their age to avoid being considered too old for certain roles, but Mickey may have confused a few other biographical details, too, more of which later.

His earliest memories were of constant rows between his mother Ann, a housewife and sometime nurse, and his father, Philip Sr., an imposing figure, an amateur bodybuilder who had held the Mr. New York title. Working as a carpenter, groundskeeper, and janitor at the local golf club, his father spent his free time either lifting weights or lifting a beer glass.

Mickey was closer to his dad and loved how big and strong he was. He loved touching his father on the upper arm as a signal to Phil, who would delight the boy by immediately then flexing his muscle. The young Mickey was a funny looking kid with big protruding ears and his appearance gave no hint that he would grow up to become a heart-throb movie star. Those ears seemed forever to be picking up the painful sound of his parents' conflict.

Phil and Ann would have many loud and violent arguments and their bust-ups often got too much for young Mickey, who would run downstairs and take sanctuary in the basement apartment of his maternal grandmother. He frequently sat on the faded couch in front of her TV set, watching his favorite show, *The Little Rascals*, with a plate of homemade cookies at his side, trying to shut the anger upstairs out of his mind.

Things eventually reached a breaking point in the marriage, with his mother and grandmother moving out and taking Mickey, his younger brother Joey, and little sister Patti with them to start a new life in Miami. The children were initially told they were just going on a sunshine vacation and their father would join them in Florida in due course.

But the night before Ann left home, Phil took Mickey aside and told him he would never be coming home because his mother was splitting up the family. The boy felt furious, let down, confused, and resentful. Unable then to grasp the complexities of adult relationships, he was extremely unhappy with his mother for taking him away. He didn't want to go but had no choice, and his mood wasn't helped when he found himself moving from motel to motel after their arrival in Miami.

His mother eventually took over a Laundromat there and the family lived in the back rooms. Mickey started at a new school nearby but had no interest in lessons and spent his time daydreaming rather than studying. He missed his dad and often kept with him an old black-and-white photograph of Phil in a bodybuilding pose – both arms raised and muscles pumped. It was the only glimpse of his father he would have for two decades.

As if the new surroundings weren't unsettling enough, just a year after the big move his now divorced mother got married again, to a widowed police detective named Gene Addis, who provided Mickey with five older stepbrothers. But Mickey didn't want anyone taking his father's place. "A year…a year!" he would say incredulously. He is ashamed to say that he gradually came to call Gene "Daddy," but theirs wasn't a happy relationship.

When he was eight years old, his class mates were all making Valentine cards to take home to their parents and Mickey got so upset that his teacher eventually told him he didn't have to write "To Dad" on his.

The joining of the Addis and Rourke clans sounded like the set-up in the classic TV sitcom *The Brady Bunch*. But the way Mickey remembers life back then, it was more like living in the Manson family. Gene was strict with him, Joey, and Patti, just as he was with his own children. But Mickey hated his tough guy ways. He quickly came to loathe his stepfather and has claimed on several occasions that he was bullied and beaten by the man he calls "the violent cop who screwed me up."

Mickey has often been close to tears when relating tales of the abuse he claims he suffered at Gene's hands, saying in various interviews it was like *Halloween 3* and that he was the victim of "nightmarish atrocities." But he refuses to say exactly what abuse he suffered – except that it wasn't sexual – and insists he will share that private information only with the therapist who has been helping him come to terms with his past.

Hitting children to keep them in line was a lot more common back then, in the 1960s, than it is in these politically correct times, but Gene Addis, who is now eighty-two, still living in Miami, and divorced from Mickey's mother, insists he was never abusive, just a strict disciplinarian. He says Mickey has exaggerated his past but he loves him, always has, and wishes he would get back in touch. But Mickey has had nothing to do with him for years and has no plans to change that state of affairs.

Mickey is also estranged from his mother, who now has Alzheimer's disease and lives in a nursing home. He could never get over how Ann would turn a blind eye and a deaf ear to his complaints about the bad treatment he was receiving from her new husband. The star cut off communication with her for a long time after he first started making money in movies and she requested that he buys her a $150,000 house. They ceased talking for good after the death of his brother Joey, who had also resented her for breaking up the family.

While his brother, who fixed motorbikes, and sister, who became a beautician, would remain in Mickey's life, that wasn't the case with his stepbrothers. He never felt close to them. As kids, the boys would sleep in the same room in triple-decker bunk beds, and whenever Mickey fell out of his top bunk, which happened a few times, his stepbrothers would laugh at him.

Their tastes were completely different, too. His stepbrothers absolutely loved wrestling and would go and watch the sport all the time. But Mickey had a terrible disdain for it and wouldn't change his mind about the sport until he starred in *The Wrestler* four decades later.

Brother Joey and sister Patti seemed to adapt better to the new environment than Mickey did. He craved the love and support of his mother but resented the way she was sharing her time and attention with her new husband and stepchildren. His grandmother was always there with a comforting arm around his shoulder or a loving smile but, apart from that, the youngster felt largely lost and bewildered. He would rather have lived in a prison than in that house.

So Mickey simply retreated and lived in his head. He felt he was living in a family that was beyond dysfunctional and remembers walking along the street one day thinking, "What am I doing living with these weird people?"

The frustration finally poured out of him when he had his first fistfight at the age of ten. In the school playground a boy came over and started kicking him. Mickey, a quiet and submissive child up until that point, suddenly snapped and started raining blows on his tormentor, giving him a severe beating. He might not have been able to strike back at home, but he decided from then on to wage war on anybody who picked on him elsewhere.

Depressed by his home life and feeling out of place at school, where he generally got *D* and *F* grades and excelled only in phys-ed, the youngster took to spending time on the streets. These were bleak times, which he refers to in interviews as "my nightmare years." Searching for the feeling of belonging he failed to find at home, young Mickey took to hanging out with a gang of hard-up local kids, started dressing the way they did, and became part of their street urchin, petty criminal lifestyle. Like his new pals, he developed a defiance of authority and a total inability to conform, which meant he was always getting into trouble, especially with the teachers at school. He got into lots of fights and once took revenge on five young thugs who had beaten up his brother Joey by hunting each of them down separately and giving them a battering in return. Mickey would continue to be protective of Joey for many years, always paying his medical bills and getting him the best treatment as his little brother fought a long battle against cancer.

But back then, Mickey was doing too much scrapping in the streets for the liking of his disciplinarian stepdad. Gene felt he needed to find another outlet for the boy's aggression. So, in a bid to keep his twelve-year-old stepson out of trouble, he signed him up for boxing lessons at Miami's world-famous Fifth Street Gym, where the great Muhammad Ali trained for his world title fights.

No matter what wrongs Gene may have done Mickey, this particular idea was a master stroke. The boy was immediately seduced by the fight scene and soon decided to take up amateur boxing. Over the next few years, he fought in the Police Athletic League, a common starting point for young American boxers, as a 146-lb welterweight, sometimes under the name Andre Rourke and other times as "Mick the Slasher." He displayed real talent for the sport and claims to have KO'ed twelve consecutive opponents in the first round on his way to compiling an amateur boxing record of twenty-seven wins – seventeen by knock-out – and just three defeats – none by being knocked out.

I say "claims" because several sources believe Mickey has exaggerated his amateur boxing achievements in Florida and the available records don't go back far enough to allow his fight statistics to be checked.

Mickey also claims to have spent part of his childhood in Liberty City, a tough Miami ghetto known back then for its slums, drugs, and riots. His stepfather, however, claims they never lived there. Local telephone directories from Mickey's teenage years place the family in a far more pleasant and affluent area of Miami, at the corner of Prairie Avenue and 47th Street.

What is undoubtedly true is that Mickey had a real passion for boxing and saw the sport as a chance to release all the anger that had been bubbling away inside him. It was around this time that he began to imagine a future for himself as a professional boxer. He had certainly learned from the best. During the five years he spent training at the Fifth Street Gym, Mickey watched Muhammad Ali at close quarters, learning many masterful moves by studying the champion that he, and many others, believe to be the greatest boxer who ever lived. He started to mimic Ali's "float like a butterfly, sting like a bee" style in the ring.

His fascination with the boxing legend continued outside the gym. He would watch Ali doing morning training runs on a nearby golf course and, at night, the teenager would go to Wolfie's Coffee Shop in South Beach and look on, star-struck, as the champ ate with fellow boxers such as Jerry Quarry and Jimmy Ellis.

Ali noticed his young fan hanging around and one day gave Mickey a much-prized present – a pair of shorts that he had worn in the ring. Young Mickey couldn't believe it. He treasured the white satin trunks with gold stripes down the side and resolved to keep the priceless gift forever. So he wasn't exactly pleased a few days later to find his mother had thrown them away because they were covered in blood. His subsequent confrontation with Ann marked the first time Mickey ever swore at his mother.

But his stepfather continued to be the main focus of his rage. Following all his workouts at the gym, Mickey had the strength and the skills to stand up to Gene. Although they continued to argue, it never ended with the future film star and fighter punching him out. The closest they came was when Mickey was sixteen and in the throes of an especially blazing row with Gene at home. His stepfather challenged Mickey to step outside and fight him like a man, but the youngster declined the invitation.

While it was the opportunity he had long wanted, Mickey reasoned that his 145-lb frame was no match for Gene, who was well over 200 lbs and, being good with his hands, could do him some serious damage in a proper fight. Mickey regrets he didn't even try to let him have it back then. It could be argued he has been unloading his anger at Gene ever since.

He went back to the gym, the one place he felt at home, and worked towards his dream of making it as a professional boxer. But his unprofessional attitude let him down. It gradually became clear that while Mickey loved the sport and possessed impressive ring skills, he just didn't have the necessary discipline and commitment. He would stay out all night getting wasted. When he went to the gym and his trainer asked if he had been out on his daily morning run, Mickey would lie, say that he had, when, in fact, he had only just stumbled in after long hours partying with pals.

It was a health scare that eventually persuaded Mickey to throw in the towel on his boxing dreams. He suffered two concussions – one while sparring in 1969 with Cuban former world welterweight champion Luis Rodriguez, and another when competing in a 1971 tournament for promising amateur fighters. Mickey was scared by what happened to him after those incidents. He would find himself standing in the street, suddenly not knowing where he was going.

After the second concussion, doctors told him to take a year off from the sport and rest. His trainer wanted him to continue with boxing after that and move to the great fighting city of Philadelphia to improve his boxing skills. But the fear of permanent brain damage put him off a career in the ring. Mickey decided to give up boxing and look for something else to do with his life.

Had he stuck with boxing, Mickey says, he would never have become an actor. But the decision to give up the sport was one he would nevertheless regret. It troubled him for years – so much so, that he would make an unlikely return to the ring two decades later.

Mickey had been a good football player at school but decided to give up that contact sport too, in view of his boxing injury. He had no future prospects, either, in the other sport in which he excelled – baseball – having blown his big chance when some big league talent scouts visited the school looking for new players.

Mickey's performance at first base had really caught several eyes – so much so that he was asked to coach a group of younger kids at Miami Beach Senior High School for a while, a job he took in order to get what he called his "Friday and Saturday night going out money." But his Little League team was very successful, thanks largely to Mickey's knowledge of the sport and to his third baseman Andy Garcia, the future movie star, who batted .600. The fact that Mickey never made the progress he should have in playing baseball was primarily due to his problem with

25

authority figures. If anyone over thirty told him to do something, he invariably wouldn't do it.

One of those authority figures was the school's senior baseball coach, the highly respected Skip Bertman, who had brought a long-hoped-for championship to the school and would go on to be voted into the sport's Hall of Fame as one of the best US school and college baseball coaches of all time.

Mickey was a gifted player, but would constantly defy Bertman's authority by provoking him and showing a lack of respect. The coach took his revenge by dropping Mickey from the team at that critical moment when the scouts descended on the school. Some people would never get over a disappointment like that, but Mickey now realizes it was his own fault and he was hurting himself with his bad attitude.

Mickey was a rebel in the way he dressed as well. Instead of the latest fashions worn by the cool kids around Miami, Mickey and his brother Joey favored flamboyant, multi-colored clothes. They would strut around like peacocks and you can imagine the kind of names they were called by the local tough kids – name calling that stopped when Joey hit one of the bigmouths with a baseball bat.

Mickey's eccentric fashion sense, which continues to this day, was raised to new and outlandish levels after he graduated from Miami Beach Senior High School in 1971. The favorite items in his closet included platform shoes, satin pants, and women's blouses, some of which were borrowed from his mother. Completing his androgynous look was the way he wore his hair then, long and dyed blond. He has no idea why he dressed like that, other than wanting to look as cool as his idol, Elvis Presley, and a feeling that he needed to fit in with his friends, who all dressed in the same way and were equally directionless as to their future prospects.

Mickey left home as soon as he could and shared rooms with three of those pals at Miami's Wild West Hotel. Given their colorful dress and close friendship, many people, not surprisingly, thought they were gay. But Mickey and his friends were into women. In fact, there was nothing else on their minds, except for maybe acting cool and getting high. They would go to the 48th Street beach all morning, get tanned and chat up babes, sleep in the afternoon, and hit the town at night, cruising around Miami, smoking joints and checking out the talent.

Mickey didn't get hooked on drugs in those beach bum days, and claims he hasn't since, despite the odd fling. Young Mickey's head was certainly clear enough to know he couldn't drift through life forever and needed to find a job. The problem was he couldn't find anything that interested him. He was too bored to remain in his job as a ditch digger for the Miami-Dade Power and Light Company and subsequently drifted into a string of other jobs – such as hotel parking lot attendant and restaurant busboy – that were short lived because he would quit in frustration or get fired for having a bad attitude. He worked at a shooting range picking up bullet casings, but had to leave that job when he developed lead poisoning.

His attempt at being an electrician lasted only a day because he couldn't figure out how to work a machine he was asked to operate and didn't like that it kept giving him electric shocks. The future film star was an usher in a movie theater for a while but lost that job when he got into a violent fight with another usher who had hit him over the head with his flashlight for fun.

Mickey was between jobs when Gary Cox, an old friend from his high school football team, approached him on the beach one day with a startling and life-altering proposition: "Would you like to give acting a try?" Gary was now going to the University of Miami and directing a play there. One of the students had dropped out and he thought Mickey would make an ideal replacement in the now vacant role, that of a brawny tough guy. Mickey pointed out that he didn't go to the University of Miami, but his pal said that didn't matter because no one would notice.

Mickey hadn't shown any interest in acting back at Miami Beach Senior High School, unlike fellow pupils and future film stars Ellen Barkin and the aforementioned Andy Garcia, who were in lower grades. But he had developed an interest in watching movies ever since his English teacher, Zelda Glazer, showed him the first film he ever saw, *A Place in the Sun*. She screened the 1951 classic twice for her class of underachievers, which included Mickey, and he remembers being fascinated by the performance of leading man Montgomery Clift. Another film that fascinated him as a child was *Mutiny on the Bounty*, starring Marlon Brando. In 2010, that inspirational teacher's writer-director son, Mitch Glazer, gave Mickey the lead role in *Passion Play*.

But Mickey's acting career might never have happened at all had the youngster not agreed, with little else to do, to check out Gary Cox's play by attending a rehearsal. *Deathwatch* by Jean Genet was about three prison inmates vying for leadership of their cell. Mickey got up on stage to read the role of Green

Eyes, one of the prisoners, was immediately hooked on acting, and agreed to do the show. He recalled, "I really liked it. I don't think I was very good, you know, but it was like, hey, this is a great feeling. Whatever this is, this is neat."

Mickey repeated the role at another local theater, enjoyed himself even more, thought it was the most worthwhile thing he had done in quite some time, and began to think acting could be the career for him. He reasoned, "I pretty much lived in my mind anyway. I thought it would be real nice to be in a different place, to be somebody else, and I needed to do something else." That was because his career options had come down to either acting or crime. His friends told him crime offered much greater guarantees of making money.

Mickey gave the gangster life a try, becoming a driver for some tough types and mixing with acquaintances who had graduated from petty crime to more serious activities. When Mickey accompanied them on a drug deal one day, he found himself caught up in a gunfight as bullets suddenly whizzed by his head. He was smart enough to realize that sticking with this line of work could get him killed.

Acting seemed a much safer option and an opportunity presented itself when a theater company in Chicago offered Mickey an apprenticeship, saying he could learn to act while making scenery. But he turned it down because he wasn't interested in building sets. He also eventually admitted to not being able to hammer a nail, so he went back to hanging out at the beach with his friends and wondering if there was an easier way to break into acting. Gary Cox, who cast him in *Deathwatch*, and went on to work as a waiter, had suggested he move to New York, which is where people went to become actors. It was certainly something to consider.

It was during a long talk about the future with one of his closest friends, Stoney Curtis – so named because he looked like Tony Curtis and loved getting stoned – that he came up with a firm plan. Mickey announced to his pal, "I'm gonna move to New York and become an actor there."

So that's what he did. He said goodbye to his colorful Miami friends – who presented him with a going away present of a baseball bat to use to ward off troublemakers in New York – got on a plane for the first time in his life, and with $400 in his pocket, which was borrowed from his sister Patti who was working at the local McDonald's, headed off to a hopefully bright future.

Looking for somewhere to stay in the Big Apple, he visited a number of addresses of people his grandmother used to know, only to find they had moved away or the buildings weren't even there anymore. One place he did know existed was the world-famous Actors' Studio where he had heard that one of his favorite movie stars, Steve McQueen, had studied. So he picked up his suitcases, got in a cab and headed there. Mickey walked in, told the people inside that he had come to New York to be an actor but had little cash and no place to stay. They were nice enough to recommend some cheap hotels favored by a lot of starving actors. He tried the Albert first and then the Earl before settling on a $38-a-week attic room at the Marlton on West 8th Street in Greenwich Village. That's where he would stay for the next few years.

Nervous about some of the bizarre characters he had seen in the hotel, Mickey took his baseball bat to bed with him every night. For the first month, he felt shy and alone. He knew nobody in the big city. Meanwhile, he had no money other than his accommodation expenses and would occasionally steal candy bars just to survive.

Things improved when a friend from Miami, Little Eddie, joined him at the Marlton. While Mickey had come to the Big Apple to be an actor, his friend's dream was to become a gangster. But with neither of those positions immediately available, they went out to look for other work together and both got jobs for a while working as attendants at a nearby parking lot.

Little Eddie was a 4ft-8in-tall Cuban whose toughness had been almost legendary in Miami. He was such a fearless character that he once stood up in a movie theater, where several other filmgoers were loudly talking during the picture, and demanded that everyone should sit down and shut the fuck up. They did.

Little Eddie had used the McDonald's where Patti Rourke worked as his unofficial office. Mickey went storming in there one day to confront him after one of his other friends had been beaten up by the tiny tough guy. When he demanded to know why he'd done it, the Cuban coolly replied, "Because he's a punk." Mickey thought about it, realized his pal *was* a punk, and decided he liked this weird little character. They became firm friends from that moment and Eddie always backed him up – once even coming to his rescue when four much bigger guys were beating up Mickey in the street.

The Cuban shared Mickey's bizarre fashion sense, too, and

31

when they found themselves together in New York, the compadres from Miami broke out the old extravagant outfits. They made quite a sight walking along together through Greenwich Village in their glam rock gear, Little Eddie on the sidewalk and Mickey in the street to minimize the height difference whenever a girl went past. They had a fun time until Little Eddie moved away to Connecticut, much to Mickey's disappointment.

With his friend gone, Mickey would hit the town alone in his brightly colored clothes, looking like a David Bowie wannabe, and was soon fighting off advances from the neighborhood homosexuals who presumed he was trawling for sex. He recalled in a later magazine interview, "I was so fucking naïve walking around in my Cuban high-heeled shoes and my fucking stardust outfit that I didn't realize the cool boys on the corner were eyeballing me because they wanted to get down."

Mickey thought he looked so cool and well dressed that one day he walked into the Ford Modeling Agency and asked for a job. He didn't get past the receptionist who looked at him as if he were nuts. But he really did need some kind of paying work if he was to survive in the big city. Thoughts of acting seemed to be forgotten as he bounced from one bizarre job to another. One of the oddest jobs he took was as an attack-dog agitator, wearing a skimpy leather patch on his arm and encouraging Doberman Pinschers to sink their teeth into it as part of their guard dog training. "That was one of my favorite ones," he laughed, "provoking a killer dog."

He also worked for the brothels on 42nd Street, supervising the team of young men from Puerto Rico who handed out flyers on the street by making sure they did their job and didn't get beaten up or chased off by pimps. He then lost his job parking cars at a valet service because he kept crashing them as he struggled to back the vehicles into tiny spaces.

All these low-paid jobs provided valuable life experience which would later be poured into his acting when he came to play characters with the odds stacked against them. Other actors who find work straight out of school for a teen series or soap opera never get that kind of insight.

But Mickey wasn't thinking back then about how lucky he was. Instead, he was battling just to scrape together enough money to pay for the fast food, potato chips, and chocolate bars which made up his diet. He knew nothing about nutrition back then and his teeth were rotting. He was also struggling to pay his bill at the rundown hotel where he was living. His grandmother would send him a few dollars each month, and the cash was vital to Mickey, who would show up hours early at the Western Union office waiting to get his check.

It was a lonely time for Mickey with no close buddies around and no girlfriend. He was shy around the big city girls and didn't know how to talk to them. They certainly didn't come running as they would when he became famous. When he did hook up with women, they looked nothing like the glamorous models and actresses who would later choose to spend time with him.

His life back then was as much a mess as was his room at the Marlton, which looked as rough as some of the girls he took back to it. The chambermaids would sometimes refuse to clean the room because it was left in such squalor. With little cash, direction, or prospects, it seemed a hopeless situation. But hope was about to walk into Mickey's life in the form of a kindly man who put him on the right track.

The great philosopher Albert Schweitzer once said, "Sometimes our light goes out but is blown again into flame by an encounter with another human being. Each of us owes the deepest thanks to those who have rekindled this inner light." Mickey owed his thanks to the night manager at the Marlton, Carl Montgomery, who befriended him and made him think seriously again about becoming an actor. Carl was a huge theater buff who would talk with great enthusiasm to the young hotel guest about the plays and performers he had seen. He gave Mickey books and articles about acting and actors, plays by Shakespeare and Tennessee Williams, recommended old films for him to watch and really reignited his interest in acting. Mickey immersed himself in this fascinating new world.

Countless actors had passed through the hotel's doors over the years but Montgomery saw something in Mickey the others never had – star quality. He just didn't know if Mickey had the dedication to make it.

Inspired by his chats with Carl, Mickey went back to the Actors' Studio, determined to win a place at the school where past students had included James Dean, Marlon Brando, and Montgomery Clift – all actors Mickey had learned more about and become a bigger fan of after the Marlton's night manager had widened his horizons. He learned that those legends, along with more recent students like Robert De Niro and Al Pacino, had studied the Stanislavski "method" there, an introspective style of performance originated by a Russian theater revolutionary in which the actor puts his own life experience into the role to bring more depth, detail, and reality to the character. That sounded good to Mickey. But he wasn't going to be able to just walk into a place at this ultimate acting school. It received thousands of applications each year and only took in a handful of students at a time.

Mickey realized he wasn't good enough yet to gain acceptance but, showing a dedication which had been missing from the rest of his life, he resolved to get the skills to make it in there someday soon, and set about that ambition by signing up for private lessons with one of the Studio's top teachers, Sandra Seacat.

At first, Sandra didn't know what to make of him. He was fascinating in his eccentricity but seemed so withdrawn and lacking in logic she even wondered if he might be a little retarded. Using all her experience in bringing out talent, however, she gradually began to figure out Mickey and put him on the path to acting greatness. She found a way to channel all the frustration in his life into his performances. The breakthrough came when she gave him a "sensory" acting exercise to do – picturing himself in a place where he was happy. Mickey imagined himself back at the Fifth Street Gym, lacing up his boxing boots and remembering the sounds and smells of the place. Then Sandra had him perform an acting scene. It allowed him to understand how to make a personal connection with the material – an acting technique he still uses to this day.

Mickey later recalled, "As I was acting this, something just clicked. All the things that had been holding me back for years started coming out – the disappointment in sports, my sadness about never having got to know my father, everything fell into place. From that day on, it was like I'd finally stopped posing and become myself, a real person."

Mickey added at one of our Q&As, "I wanted to be the best actor I possibly could be. With the boxing it had never been 100 per cent but suddenly acting was. I had no social life. I studied like a monk. I would grab bums off the street to run lines with me at night."

Seeing that level of commitment, drama coach Sandra Seacat felt it was time for Mickey to audition for a place at the Actors' Studio. It was preparing for that big test which forced Mickey to take a journey he might otherwise never have – a visit to his father.

His audition scene for the Studio was from the Tennessee Williams play *Cat on a Hot Tin Roof,* the one in which Brick discusses his drinking problem with his father, Big Daddy. While rehearsing it, Mickey wasn't able to make the father-and-son relationship convincing. He talked it over with Seacat and she said he would continue to have a problem with that scene, and similar ones in the future, unless he got to know his own father. She advised her student to go and find his dad and talk to him.

Mickey was reluctant. He hadn't had any contact with Phil since his parents parted all those years before. But he was still holding on to that treasured photograph of his father in bodybuilding pose. Although Mickey wasn't keen to find out how time had changed his dad, his determination to improve his acting and win a place at the Actors' Studio was a powerful motivator and provided him with the courage to get on a bus to Schenectady.

The moment he arrived in town, Mickey noticed the White Castle diner on State Street where, as a child, he had enjoyed milkshakes with his father. He decided to go in and have one for old time's sake. As he stepped inside, his attention was immediately drawn to a middle-aged man, sitting alone, wearing glasses. He certainly didn't look like a bodybuilder, but it was unmistakably Phil Rourke. Mickey recognized him because of his hands – which looked just like his. He also had the same forehead and mouth.

Mickey froze and couldn't approach him. But when Phil got up and walked out, Mickey followed him outside. He walked up to him, took a deep breath and said, "Are you Phil? I'm Mickey." The man fixed his glasses halfway down his nose, looked at the young man standing in front of him, and replied, "Is your mother here?" His son shook his head. Phil looked disappointed for a second, then he stared at Mickey, paused, and said, "I always knew you'd come to see me one day."

Father and son then went to a place nearby where Phil bought Mickey a dinner of pork chops, mashed potatoes, and sauerkraut and nervously drank many screwdrivers while watching him eat. Gradually, the conversation started to flow. Mickey kept saying things like, "Dad, would you pass the salt?" and "Dad, shall we get another drink?" so his father would know he still called him "Dad."

In another emotional moment, he touched his dad's upper arm just like he used to do when he was a kid – but this time there was no muscle there, the skin was just soft. Mickey felt his stomach lurch. He couldn't believe this was the same powerfully built man whose picture he had been carrying around for the past seventeen years.

He told Phil about the Actors' Studio and was surprised to find his father also had an interest in theater. Phil had once reviewed plays for an army newspaper when he was stationed in Germany as a young man. It upset Mickey that they had not been able to share this passion and had missed out on so many years together. Suddenly, he felt uncomfortable and got up to leave, but Phil pulled him back for one last drink – and did the same thing a couple of more times.

Eventually, it was time for the last bus back to New York and, before Mickey got on board, Phil thrust $50 into his son's hand and said, "Take it, you'll break my heart if you don't." Then he suddenly embraced Mickey with a bear hug and started to cry.

During the bus journey back, young Mickey realized he felt less detached from his dad. But his thoughts drifted away from their emotional reunion and back to the *Cat on a Hot Tin Roof* scene he would have to perform for the audition panel the next morning. During the late night bus ride and the eventual walk back to his room, Mickey wasn't wearing warm enough clothes. He shivered all the way home as he tried to relate what he had just experienced in Schenectady to the acting task ahead.

The next day, as he nervously paced outside the audition room preparing for the make or break performance, he couldn't summon up those same feelings of awkwardness about his father. So, moments before he was due on stage, he rushed outside into the New York snow and took off his shirt to re-experience the bitter cold he had felt the previous night. It served to put him in the same state of mind he had been feeling then. Mickey was now ready to audition.

He blew away the panel with a performance of stunning realism, playing the scene as if he were talking to his own big daddy rather than the character. On the panel was Actors' Studio co-founder Elia Kazan, three-time Oscar-winning director of such classic films as *On the Waterfront* and *East of Eden*, who said Mickey's piece was the best audition he had seen in thirty years.

It was a proud moment for Sandra Seacat, who continues to be a mentor to emerging actors and recently discovered Star Trek's new Captain Kirk, Chris Pine. The audition was a triumph for Mickey who was immediately offered that coveted place at the Actors' Studio and eagerly accepted. Thousands had applied that year. Rourke was one of only five who got in. Jack Nicholson had needed five auditions before he made it into the Studio, Dustin Hoffman, six. It had taken Harvey Keitel eleven tries. Mickey did it in one.

But there was no happy ending to the story of him and his father. They did keep in touch after their reunion and Phil would write him letters every so often. But they never met again. Phil passed away just a few years later, aged just forty-nine. "He drank himself to death," said Mickey.

Getting into the Actors' Studio, which he calls "a sacred place," was a dream come true for Mickey, but you wouldn't know it from the way he behaved. He was shy, nervous, and quiet around the students and staff. For his first two years, he would just sit in a corner listening, too terrified to make a significant contribution in class.

Mickey would watch mesmerized as the likes of Christopher Walken, Harvey Keitel and Al Pacino – who were all making the step up from students to stars at the time – would stop by the Actors' Studio to hone their craft and seemingly have the ability to tap into different emotions at a moment's notice. He remembers being star struck the first time he came face to face there with Keitel, whose work he had admired in the 1973 film *Mean Streets*. Keitel snapped his fingers at Mickey to get him to move out of his way. Mickey said of those stars, "They had set the bar high and I wanted to be like them, to be that kind of actor."

But it wasn't easy. Although opening up his emotions had landed him a place, he was too embarrassed to get up in front of the class and talk in public about his feelings. Yet he did enjoy the improvisation exercises and gradually started to flourish when hiding behind characters he would make up on the spot.

Tuition didn't come cheap and Mickey had to take another succession of short-lived jobs so he could continue paying for his classes. He was often fired and always broke but forever on the lookout for a shot at the big time. Unlike so many other acting students, he couldn't get a job as a waiter because his math skills weren't good enough. For a time, he moved furniture in the same warehouse where Gene Hackman, Steve McQueen and Lee Marvin had all worked before getting their big breaks.

One job Mickey was able to hold down for a while was selling food from a cart at the side of Central Park close to the big casting agencies. He would sell pretzels and chestnuts in the winter and ice cream in the summer but, whatever the time of year, he always kept a pair of sunglasses in his pocket ready to whip out whenever someone who looked like a casting director walked past.

The tactic didn't lead to him getting any acting work. In fact, Mickey took five years of classes before he actively went looking for acting jobs. It was his mentor Sandra Seacat, who would continue to be a great support to him as he built a film career, who finally persuaded him to leave. She felt he was becoming part of the furniture at the Actors' Studio and told him so in no uncertain terms. Sandra yelled at him out in the street, "Do you want to take classes for the rest of your life? Get out there and work."

So Mickey tried to do just that. He looked for roles in off-Broadway experimental theater and was hired, largely on the back of his impressive training. But he quit most shows during rehearsals as his old problems with authority figures returned and he clashed with the directors. If the play wasn't going the way he wanted, he would be gone. It seemed being part of a theater company just wasn't for him.

Mickey got his first screen acting role in the 1976 short film *Love in the Hamptons*. He had the lead role of Swede, a working-class young man in love with a waitress, and his dedication to authentic performances was already present. A moment before filming a scene in which his character wakes up in the morning, he threw a handful of sand in his eyes in order to create that gritty, eye-rub feeling people often have as soon as they get up. The five-day shoot went well and Mickey started to think his future lay in film rather than theater.

But movies were mostly made in Los Angeles, whereas New York was a theater town. A couple of years later, Mickey decided to try his luck in films and relocated to LA, aiming to become a star.

The bold ambition got off to a good start when was signed up for representation by John Travolta's managers, Bob LeMond and Lois Zetter, and later got a good up-and-coming agent in Bernie Carneol, who worked around the clock trying to secure auditions for him. Now Mickey just needed to land some roles. But there was a problem which would be a constant barrier to his employment, then and for years to come.

While the Actors' Studio had given him the tools to do the job, it hadn't taught him the politics of the industry and how the business worked. There had been no classes in business skills. Consequently, he had no clue how to sell himself to casting agents. All the pleasantries of kissing ass and sucking up to these people for a role were a mystery to him. Mickey also had a particular acting technique where he would wait for the right feeling to descend on him before delivering his lines. But with dozens of other actors waiting to audition for the same part, casting agents wanted him to get on with it and couldn't hang around until he was emotionally ready to perform. As a result, Mickey kept blowing the opportunities with which he was presented. He went through seventy-five auditions before he got his first part.

The only steady work he did find during that time in LA was as a bouncer in a Hollywood Boulevard transvestite club called Danielle's. He was kept busy because the customers would come in high on angel dust, which gave them a feeling of superhuman strength and led to them getting into violent fights. Mickey would try and break things up while raging trannies picked up steel napkin holders from the tables and threw them at him. One night, the other bouncer whacked one muscle-bound, high-as-a-kite transvestite over the head with a wooden club, but the club broke in half and the customer kept advancing. After that incident, Mickey quit as a bouncer but kept on working there in the slightly safer job of waiter. He couldn't turn his back on Danielle's entirely because he was getting the odd TV or film acting job here and there but never the kind of high-paying major role or regular work that would allow him to pursue acting full time.

The breakthrough opportunity finally came when he went along on his lunch break from the transvestite club to audition for a small but flashy part as a streetwise arsonist alongside William Hurt in the 1981 thriller movie *Body Heat*. This time, Mickey greatly impressed the casting agents with his audition and was offered the part – a role which would finally put him on the Hollywood map.

But instead of saying "Thanks very much" and gratefully grabbing the job with both hands, Mickey's stubborn streak returned and he insisted the moviemakers should improve their financial offer to him or he wouldn't take the role. The offer was $500 a day for two days' work, but Mickey, despite being a virtual nobody, demanded $1,000 a day.

His agent, Bernie Carneol, couldn't believe it and thought Mickey had lost his mind. In near despair, he told him, "But Mickey, you work in a transvestite club... take the offer!"

Showing an unwillingness to compromise – which would be the hallmark of his personality for years to come – Mickey held out for the extra $500 a day he felt he was worth. And he got it.

It wasn't so much that he was business savvy. Mickey just wanted everything done on his own terms as usual. This "my way or the highway" approach on *Body Heat* became a feature of his future dealings with film bosses.

Mickey made the absolute most of his opportunity in *Body Heat*, playing the part to perfection with a mix of swagger and quiet confidence. His twitchy, spellbinding performance caught the eye of Hollywood's top casting directors. He was now on his way to the Hollywood dream.

Little did he know then, it would soon turn into a nightmare.

2
A Life on Screen – Part I

Caked in make-up, smeared with thick lipstick, wearing a red bra and various other items of women's clothing while tottering along in powder-blue ladies' shoes, Mickey Rourke boarded a plane from LA to Vancouver. It was all part of his method acting approach to playing a transvestite in the 2000 movie *Animal Factory*.

Instead of waiting to get changed on the set in Canada, Mickey decided to live the role for real by donning drag for the plane journey to the filming location. The very convincing outfit had been painstakingly put together after ten days' shopping at flamboyant LA boutiques like Trashy Lingerie. He was wearing such long, fake fingernails that he struggled to pull his flight ticket out of his pocket at the boarding gate. A little boy behind him was watching in fascination. Mickey smiled down at him but the strangely dressed star didn't have in his two front teeth – which are false as a legacy of his boxing days – and the little fellow was so scared he ran and hid behind his mother's skirt.

On the flight, Mickey took his seat and noticed the other passengers staring at him. Unsettled by their attention, he developed a blotchy rash. The flight attendant came down the aisle asking passengers, "Would you like a drink, sir?" or "Would you like a drink, ma'am?" She got to Mickey, looked unsure, dispensed with both "sir" and "ma'am" and enquired, "Can I get you anything?"

When he got to the set in drag and said hello, director Steve Buscemi didn't recognize him. Eventually, the star had to say, "It's me, Mickey!" Buscemi looked aghast and replied, "Jesus Christ!"

Mickey was superb in the film – just one of many great performances he has given over the past thirty years.

* * *

It's ironic, in view of Mickey Rourke's often disappointing box-office returns, that he should have been involved in Steven Spielberg's only massive flop. Mickey's first movie credit – he's actually listed sixty-eighth in the cast list – comes as Private Reese in the 1979 movie entitled *1941*, an absurd wartime farce about Californians lapsing into a panic at the prospect of a Japanese invasion. Spielberg had intended it as a "stupidly outrageous celebration of paranoia." Well, he got the stupid part right. Audiences quite rightly ignored the movie, which starred John Belushi and Dan Aykroyd.

The only slight consolation for Mickey was that the film's failure wasn't his fault. He hung around the set for ten weeks but didn't even get an appearance in the final cut for his trouble. Mickey waited for his part to materialize, but it never did – a rough introduction to the big time.

But he did appear in a few scenes of *Fade to Black* (1980), a weird little horror movie starring Dennis Christopher as a strange young man whose obsession with movies leads him to dress up as film stars and carry out a killing spree. Mickey was eleventh on the cast list this time in the role of a bullying thug named Richie, but the movie failed to make any kind of impact.

He had high hopes for his next film, though, and with a budget of more than $50 million what could possibly go wrong? Plenty, as it turned out. The film was *Heaven's Gate* (1980), one of the biggest commercial and creative disasters of all time. A rambling western about cattlemen in old Wyoming, *Heaven's Gate* drags on for an ass-numbing 219 minutes with nothing much happening.

Mickey was thrilled to be working with director Michael Cimino and co-star Christopher Walken who, just a month before filming started, had both won Oscars for *The Deer Hunter* – a favorite of Mickey's and the only film he has watched more than three times. But his excitement got the better of him. Nerves took hold as he prepared to shoot a scene with Walken, an old acquaintance and idol of his from The Actors' Studio, and when Cimino called "Action!" Mickey froze, completely unable to say his lines.

Cimino's reaction was to take Mickey aside, call him a "dumb son of a bitch" and hit him with his hat. Mickey actually responded well to that approach, was fine from that point on, and had a lot of respect for Cimino.

He ended up bonding well with Walken, who had one of the lead roles as a hired gun while Mickey had a tiny part as one of his gun-toting sidekicks, Nick Ray, thirty-third in the credits this time. Despite getting off to a bad start, he gradually also made a good impression on director Michael Cimino, and learned a lot about the movie-making process during the twelve weeks he was on the set.

Cimino went way over budget and schedule, taking eight months to shoot the debacle. After five days on set, he was already four days behind schedule. He was determined that the film should be his unique vision and, to ensure that happened, he posted an armed security guard outside the editing room to keep executives from the film studio, United Artists, away. Its spectacular failure at the box office bankrupted United Artists, and led to a Hollywood re-think on big-budget epics. The movie cost $36 million and made back just $1 million at US theaters. Critics found the story totally incoherent and were particularly savage about Cimino, whose career suffered from the setback.

Another black mark against the movie was the scale of animal abuse that took place during production. At least four animals reportedly died on set in a film that featured horse torture, cockfights, and chicken decapitation. The outcry prompted new rules in Hollywood, with the American Humane Society brought in thereafter to monitor the use and treatment of animals in all US films and TV shows.

Mickey makes only a blink-and-you'll-miss-him appearance in the final cut of *Heaven's Gate* but the experience at least gave him time to get to know Walken and Cimino, both of whom he would go on to work with in future and in more entertaining films.

Mickey then landed his first notable film role in steamy thriller *Body Heat* (1981), playing a charismatic criminal in just a couple of scenes but stealing the movie from its stars, William Hurt and

Kathleen Turner. Director Lawrence Kasdan was looking for a young Robert De Niro and, when Mickey read for the role, it was as though the heir to that great actor had suddenly emerged.

Body Heat sees Hurt's character, a lawyer, plotting to kill his lover's husband and going to see a client, soft-spoken arsonist Teddy Lewis, for advice on how to do the deed. When Mickey, as Lewis, describes how to set a fire, he conveys everything through a quiet stillness, leaning in close, staring thoughtfully and lowering his voice as he warns his lawyer to reconsider what he's doing. It was the first of many bad boys with a conscience he would play down the years. Mickey's now familiar mannerisms and scorching talent were all on show. The film also marked the start of his long career of saying "fuck" on screen.

Many critics praised his work in their reviews of *Body Heat* and Hollywood sat up and took notice of the newcomer. The James Dean comparisons started, but Mickey, with his halting delivery of lines, was more of a rebel with a pause.

Now Mickey could quit his job at the transvestite club and sift through the film offers that started to come in as leading moviemakers clamored to work with him. Lawrence Kasdan offered Mickey a role in his next film, *The Big Chill*, but was turned down because the actor didn't want to do a film about "a whole bunch of yuppies." Instead, Mickey signed up for the comedy-drama *Diner* (1982), for which writer-director Barry Levinson assembled a cast of unknowns with the potential to become big stars.

Levinson clearly knew what he was doing because his other casting choices included Kevin Bacon and Steve Guttenberg, as well as Ellen Barkin, who had gone to the same high school in Miami as Mickey but had not known him back then. Mickey was easily the best of the bunch, showing a mix of toughness and vulnerability as girl-chasing hairdresser Boogie Sheftell.

Set in 1959, the movie follows a group of longtime friends who meet up at a Baltimore diner to discuss girls, gambling, and life in general, courtesy of some sharp, funny dialogue from Levinson, who would go on to direct *Good Morning, Vietnam* and *Rain Man*. The Baltimore diner used in the film was a real one, not a set, but is no longer in business, having re-opened twenty years later as a job training center for disadvantaged youths. Levinson based the script on the kind of pals he had hung out with while growing up. They certainly weren't the kind Mickey had grown up around – he would have found them all too boring for his taste. But his role as Boogie was a good one and Mickey really shone in his first substantial film appearance, showcasing a sweet smile and a cheeky charm as the smooth talking skirt-chaser.

Diner is best remembered for the scene in which Boogie bets his pals that he can get a beautiful blonde to touch his "pecker" on their first date at a cinema. He wins the bet by sticking it in the bottom of the popcorn box on his lap and giving her the shock of her life when she reaches in to grab a handful. Mickey's real acting genius, though, comes in the next scene where he convinces the startled bimbo to forgive him by spinning her a tall tale that it was all an innocent accident caused when his excitement at sitting next to her got the better of him.

While his acting instincts were spot on, the same couldn't be said for his make-up choices. On *Diner*, Mickey insisted on doing his own eye make-up – because Christopher Walken had once told him that's what he always did. So Mickey pulled out his own make-up kit and set to work. The odd results can be seen in various scenes. Eventually, the director of photography pulled him aside one day and told him to let the professionals do it instead, saying, "Listen, we're not doing *Dracula*."

As good as he was in the film, Mickey wasn't especially wild at the time about *Diner* or any of his colleagues. But he was enthusiastic to be teaming up with Nicolas Roeg, a director he greatly admired, on his next film, *Eureka* (1983). Mickey had always gone to Roeg films, such as *Don't Look Now* and *The Man Who Fell to Earth*, on the first day they came out. So he jumped at the opportunity to work on the moviemaker's latest complex drama, especially as part of the filming was to be done in Jamaica, which sounded like a great place to combine business with pleasure.

Eureka is the story of a troubled billionaire, played by Gene Hackman, battling mobsters who want to open a casino on the Caribbean island he owns. Mickey, in thick-rimmed glasses and with slicked back hair, plays Aurelio D'Amato, a lawyer working for a Mafia boss, who has been sent round to make the tycoon an offer he can't refuse. Mickey didn't care for the part, but did enjoy being around Roeg and was amused when the director would anger some of the other actors by telling them how to say their lines properly. In the end, few people ended up seeing *Eureka*, which opened in only a handful of cinemas around the world before quickly disappearing.

Mickey then found a role to sink his teeth into with *Rumble*

Fish (1983), Francis Ford Coppola's visually stunning adaptation of the Susie Hinton novel about troubled youths in Tulsa. A huge fan of the director's masterpiece *The Godfather*, Mickey had eagerly auditioned for a role in Coppola's previous film, *The Outsiders*, and while he hadn't been right for that one – he was too old for a film about teenage gangs – the director was hugely impressed with the newcomer and decided to cast him as the enigmatic older brother, Motorcycle Boy, in his next picture.

Mickey was so grateful and determined to please Coppola that he resolved to give the performance everything he had. His dedication to certain roles first showed itself on this film. To prepare for playing such a weird character, Mickey dyed his hair red and wore bright green contact lenses – even though the movie was shot in black and white. What impressed Coppola more was the subtle way Mickey managed to make his character so charismatic despite having few lines. It was all due to an acting technique he had never witnessed before or since.

Each day, Mickey would come to him with an object, such as a ring, a stone, or some other amulet, show it to the director, and then put it in his pocket. For the rest of the day while filming scenes, he would focus his thoughts on the object in his pocket rather than on the lines he was saying or what was happening in the scene. That approach most likely came from reading some advice about acting for the screen once given by Marlon Brando who said, "You can't care or they'll see it in your face." In other words, if the actor is concentrating on something else, rather than the action in the scene, then the performance will feel more natural because, in real life, people are so often doing one thing while thinking about something else.

Mickey's part gave him plenty to think about, and a lot to relate to as Motorcycle Boy has an alcoholic father, a younger brother he adores, and resents his mother for moving away when he was very young. While the film was being made in Tulsa, Mickey received the devastating news that his brother had been diagnosed with cancer – the first of many bouts Joey would have with the disease.

To further personalize the performance, the photograph Mickey's character uses as a bookmark – which is supposed to show Motorcycle Boy as a toddler with a protective arm around his brother when he was a baby – was actually an old photo of Mickey and Joey Rourke. It can be seen in close-up at one point in the movie.

The bond of brothers was what appealed most to Francis Ford Coppola about the story. He had always looked up to his own dapper and handsome older brother, August, to whom the film is dedicated. *Rumble Fish* marks the movie acting debut of August's son, Nicolas Cage – or Nicolas Coppola, as he was then credited – who plays tough guy Smoky and wears one of his dad's old jackets in the film.

Aside from Cage, the movie featured several other young cast members who would go on to big things – Diane Lane, Larry Fishburne, and, in the role of Motorcycle Boy's younger brother Rusty James, Matt Dillon. But it's Mickey who stands out from the pack, not just for his world-weary performance but for his look, too. Instead of wearing the traditional moody movie biker outfit of black leather, his character dresses in a very different, more sophisticated way, a look Coppola says was inspired by the French philosopher Albert Camus. He had given Mickey some Camus novels and a biography of Napoleon to help him prepare for the role.

Because Motorcycle Boy is color-blind, the movie is shot almost entirely in black and white. The only color in the film is provided by the two exotic fish which give the movie its title. If you put two Rumble Fish – or Siamese Fighting Fish – in the same tank they will fight until one kills the other. Mickey's character is killed at the end – the first of many times he would die in the closing moments of movies – after he and his brother free the fish and all the other pets from a pet shop.

Coppola ranks *Rumble Fish* as one of the best films he has ever made, but it became, along with the musical *One from the Heart*, one of the least financially successful movies of his whole career.

The first time Mickey remembers being disenchanted with the film business was when *Rumble Fish* was not well received on release. As Mickey had found with *Heaven's Gate*, and earlier with *1941*, a much lauded director was now being laughed at for making a risky project. But Mickey wasn't amused.

His mood wouldn't have been lightened by the largely negative reviews for his own performance, which was such a trademark display of method acting that several critics suggested the movie would have been more appropriately called "Mumble Fish."

But his spirits were lifted by his next film, *The Pope of Greenwich Village* (1984), which provided Mickey with the most fun he ever had on a movie. It was the first of three films in a row he was to make that were set in New York and he was thrilled to be back on the streets of his favorite city. But the biggest thrill came from co-starring with Eric Roberts, whom he calls "the best actor I ever worked with."

Few actors can steal scenes from Mickey Rourke but Roberts at least matches him all the way in this thoroughly entertaining tale of two cousins who steal a safe full of Mob money and get into big trouble with both the cops and the Mafia.

The film was originally due to star acting greats Al Pacino and Robert De Niro, but Mickey and Roberts proved more than able replacements. Eric's role was the wayward cousin Paulie, while Mickey starred as the smarter, more sophisticated cousin, Charlie Moran, and he spent $10,000 of his own money buying elegant clothes for his sharply dressed character to wear in the film. He also prepared for the part by spending three months hanging out in the dive bars of Greenwich Village, getting to meet the patrons, Mob guys, and local characters. But his dedication to duty would best be shown once the cameras started rolling.

One scene called for Mickey to have a blazing row with his on-screen girlfriend, played by Daryl Hannah, which ended with her punching him hard in the face. Daryl connected so well that she knocked a cap off one of Mickey's teeth. Mickey didn't mind but he was glad when director Stuart Rosenberg, who had previously made *Cool Hand Luke* and *The Amityville Horror*, chose not to ask for a second take.

Pope wasn't a hit but won good reviews and has many fans. Johnny Depp loves the movie and calls it "perfect cinema." A main reason the movie still holds up well today is the interplay between Rourke and Roberts. In February 2009, when he was named Best

Actor for *The Wrestler* at the Independent Spirit Awards, Mickey used his acceptance speech to pay tribute to his *Pope of Greenwich Village* co-star and urged the moviemakers present to give Eric Roberts a second shot at stardom, just as he had been given.

Mickey's next shot at acting greatness was to come with his biggest role to date, the lead in crime thriller *Year of the Dragon* (1985). He played crusading cop Stanley White, bravely waging a one-man war against the Chinese Mafia in New York. The movie marked Michael Cimino's return to directing after the *Heaven's Gate* fiasco, and he and Mickey got to work with a well-crafted script by Oliver Stone which blurred the lines of good and evil.

Crowds flocked to cinemas when the movie opened in America in the late summer of 1985, but they weren't fighting to get in. Instead, they were protesting against its showing. The film was slammed by politicians and activists for alleged racism and violence in its depiction of New York's Chinese community. The critics slaughtered the film, too, much to Mickey's dismay. He felt the poor reviews had nothing to do with the movie but, instead, were a backlash against Michael Cimino, who had become a punching bag for the press since *Heaven's Gate*.

Year of the Dragon was a commercial and critical failure, but Mickey found that hard to take at the time, saying, "The critics who destroyed that picture are the scum of the earth. May they burn in hell – and you can put that down." He was so distraught that he seriously considered quitting the movie business there and then and launching a new career by opening a motorbike shop. It sounded more appealing than exposing himself to more aggravation. Mickey felt especially hurt because he had put so much work into the performance, researching the role by spending three months shadowing a real cop called Stanley White – whom his character is named after, in thanks – and going out on homicide calls with him. Mickey had also worked hard to develop a completely different look in that film, and dyed his hair grey because his character was supposed to be much older than he was.

But his younger and sexier look in his next film would make him one of the most desired men on the planet. Mickey lost weight, got in shape, and had a neat haircut for the erotic drama *9½ Weeks* (1986), the movie that really put him on the map. The screenplay was based on a book of the same name, supposedly a memoir of her own erotic experiences by New Yorker Elizabeth McNeill, which, it later emerged, was the pen name of a half-Swedish, half-French woman called Ingebord Day.

Mickey played rich, mysterious, and dangerous stockbroker John who seduces up-for-it art gallery assistant Elizabeth, played by Kim Basinger, into a series of kinky sex games. From the moment they first meet, she is putty in his hands. The guilty pleasure of a film is full of steamy scenes like their quickie in the clock tower, her crawling across the floor picking up money and, most memorably, the food orgy. In that scene, John orders Elizabeth to close her eyes and slide down to the kitchen floor in front of his open refrigerator. He then tantalizes her tongue with food – strawberries, jelly, peppers, pasta, then Vicks cough syrup and milk.

Hundreds of actresses had been seen for the role of Elizabeth, who falls under John's erotic spell, before the moviemakers settled

57

on relative newcomer Basinger, who had broken into movies three years earlier as the Bond girl Domino in Sean Connery's *Never Say Never Again*. The stunning blonde was considered to have the perfect look and personality for the part.

Although Mickey and Kim generated real erotic heat on screen – so much so that they were voted the sexiest movie couple ever in a 2008 survey – their relationship was colder off camera. She didn't like his smoking habit and called him "the human ashtray." Neither was she amused by Mickey's habit of blasting his favorite Billy Idol song, "Rebel Yell," at full volume on set right before takes in order to help him get into character.

But Kim and Mickey never really got to know each other – and that was a deliberate choice. Director Adrian Lyne didn't want them to meet before filming so that they would be more convincing when meeting as strangers in the movie. In fact, the first time Mickey laid eyes on Basinger was just before filming the scene in the Chinese butcher shop where their characters encounter each other for the first time. They kept their distance during the rest of filming, too, and, despite being so intimate on screen, had virtually no relationship off camera. It would be twenty-three years before they would meet again.

To research his financial trader role, Mickey went to Wall Street and the New York Stock Exchange, and hated every minute of his visit. He reflected he would rather dig ditches again than work there. Mickey thought long and hard about his own look in the film and went out and bought $12,000 worth of suits he thought his character would wear in the movie.

Adrian Lyne took one look at them and said, "Mate, they're

all wrong." He said they were too flashy for a stockbroker and more appropriate to the character he had played in *The Pope of Greenwich Village*. Instead of taking them back to the shop, Mickey kept them all for himself, wearing instead the Brooks Brothers suits the costume department came up with for the film. He wanted to have spiky hair in the film like Billy Idol, but Lyne wanted it flatter, and there were regular disputes because whenever the on-set hairdresser styled his hair, Mickey would run off to the bathroom and spike it up in front of the mirror and return with his newly primped hair ready for filming.

Director Lyne, as he had proved with his earlier movie *Flashdance*, has a great visual style and the movie had a terrific, atmospheric look, like one of the finest 1980s pop videos. One scene was atmospheric to the detriment of Mickey's health. So much blue smoke was pumped around the chic boutique in the scene where John buys Elizabeth a dress that Mickey developed a bronchial problem and was off sick for two days.

Mickey liked the director, but didn't feel the finished movie went far enough, thinking the sadomasochism angle could have been pushed much further. Basinger didn't share his opinion but Mickey had hoped to be able to contribute to an all-out erotic masterpiece, bolder than anything in Brando's *Last Tango in Paris*, and didn't like the compromises in the final cut.

But plenty of people were perfectly happy with *9½ Weeks*: Mickey became an international star on the film's release. And his growing fan base eagerly awaited the idol's next move.

But Mickey was prepared to keep them waiting. Hurt by the critical slaying of *Year of the Dragon* and the safe editing of *9½*

Weeks, he was disillusioned with the business, in no rush to get back in front of the cameras, and prepared to sit it out until a masterpiece came his way. He took a year off, spending lots of money, giving lots away, and very quickly the cash started to run out. Mickey realized he had to get back to work – and needed to grab the best script available.

Mickey Rourke was one of four actors under consideration for the lead role in supernatural thriller *Angel Heart* (1987). But when he met with director Alan Parker in LA to discuss the film, he managed to convince him that only he could play the part and so there was no point talking to the other contenders. Parker knew about Mickey's growing reputation for not showing up for work on time and being difficult with directors, so he hired him on the condition that his leading man act with total professionalism.

While Mickey knew that the role of private detective Harry Angel was a good one, the greater motivation for wanting the job was a desire to keep his expensive Beverly Hills house. Mickey had been spending money like crazy and realized that the large *Angel Heart* pay check would enable him to keep up his $25,000-a-month mortgage payments and pay off various other bills.

Rich in dark atmosphere, gorgeously shot, and brilliantly acted by Mickey, *Angel Heart* is arguably Mickey's best film – at least until *The Wrestler* came along two decades later.

Set in 1955, it sees his private-eye character hired by a sinister man called Louis Cyphre (the clue is in the name) to track down a former client named Johnny Favorite who owes him something but has mysteriously disappeared. Harry's manhunt leads from New York to New Orleans, past a trail of dead bodies, into a romance with a young voodoo princess called Epiphany Proudfoot, and ends with a creepy and shocking twist.

Mickey had a series of ideas for his character, including giving him a giant fake nose, jet-black hair and a limp, each of which Parker rejected.

The best scenes in the film are the ones between Mickey and Robert De Niro, who played Louis Cyphre – a chilling role that almost went instead to Marlon Brando. Mickey relished the opportunity to share the screen with one of the true acting greats and someone he hugely respected. He learned a lot from seeing just how focused and disciplined De Niro was – two qualities Mickey had struggled with ever since his amateur boxing days. He was determined to show he had great skills, too, and seeing them square off is almost like watching two heavyweight boxing legends battling for supremacy. One acting trick Mickey used to create the right level of fear to film an encounter with his co-star's creepy character was to imagine himself being eight years old again and having to face his terrifying stepfather. And to help him feel the tension while filming their climactic scene, Mickey clutched an ice cube in his fist. By the time it was completed, there was a puddle next to his feet. Mickey still keeps on his wall at home a photo he had taken on the set with De Niro.

Parker loved Mickey's work with De Niro, but the director had to rein him in during his scene with Charlotte Rampling, in the role of Margaret Krusemark. She was word perfect on every take but Mickey would go off script and improvise new lines each time in a bid to find a fresh way to play the scene. Parker felt the best way to do the scene was by delivering the words that were written and firmly told his star to stick to the script. The director would eventually call Mickey "a nightmare" to work with because of his unpredictability, but he admired his acting genius at the same time.

In the scene near the end of the film when Harry Angel confronts Ethan Krusemark and reacts violently when much of the terrible truth is explained to him, Mickey was, accidentally, a little too violent. It called for him to clamp ice tongs to the side of the head of actor Stocker Fontelieu, who was playing Krusemark, but it turned out the rusty tongs were still quite sharp and blood started trickling from Stocker's temples. Alan Parker suddenly remembered he hadn't asked for any theatrical blood and quickly called cut so the actor could get attention. They abandoned the scene immediately and picked it up again a couple of days later, by which time the ice tongs had been blunted before they were handed over to Mickey.

On its release, the film became best known for its controversial sex scene between Mickey's character and Epiphany Proudfoot, played by Lisa Bonet, who at the time was starring in TV's most successful and most wholesome sitcom, *The Cosby Show*. Seeing her romp naked amid a shower of blood with Mickey's character, who it is later revealed is her father, was almost too much for the US ratings board and Mickey had to make a personal plea, along with Alan Parker, in front of the censors before the film – with a crucial few seconds cut from the bloody bonk scene – was eventually cleared for release in the States.

Angel Heart made Mickey appear even more iconic and cool. *9½ Weeks* director Adrian Lyne said that if Mickey had died after

Angel Heart, he would have instantly become as famous as James Dean.

All of Hollywood's top scripts were now coming his way, but Mickey, who had by now developed an attitude, refused to listen to advice from his agents or anyone else. He turned down the major movies and, instead, made his own vanity projects. His next roles would be an IRA gunman in *A Prayer for the Dying*, a shambling alcoholic in *Barfly*, a washed-up boxer in a film he wrote himself, *Homeboy*, a disfigured criminal in *Johnny Handsome* and even St Francis of Assisi in *Francesco*. All the films flopped and served to derail Mickey's promising career.

Mickey took half his usual salary to star as a disillusioned IRA terrorist in the low-budget thriller *A Prayer for the Dying* (1987) because he believed in the project and thought it would be a serious examination of the Irish Troubles. But he soon learned that producer Samuel Goldwyn Jr. had a different vision for the film and saw it as a conventional action movie with plenty of gunfire and killings.

The pair clashed repeatedly, with Goldwyn telling Mickey that his Northern Irish accent was too thick and hard to understand. That hurt Mickey, who had worked for four months with dialogue coach Brendan Gunn to come up with a speaking voice so convincing that you would believe he had been born in a field of shamrocks. On day one of filming, he had the line, "If you're dead, does it matter?" With his accent, it sounded like, "If yer da'ed, does it motter?" One of Goldwyn's representatives came over to ask why he had to say it like that, and the problems only got worse from that point. The producer also felt that Mickey's performance could be more upbeat and less lethargic, and that he would like his character to shoot more people.

Mickey's frustration and anger with the way the film was going was plain to see when Jack Higgins – author of the novel on which the movie was based – asked him for an autograph for his then sixteen-year-old daughter, Hannah, and Mickey wrote: "To Hannah – we all know it's a pile of crap, Mickey."

The whole shoot was a stressful experience for the actor who got through it only by listening to relaxation tapes he had flown over from California. Nevertheless, he managed to turn in a fine performance as gunman Martin Fallon who wants out of the killing business but is pursued for his services by a ruthless gangster, played by Alan Bates, and an IRA associate, played by Liam Neeson. Bob Hoskins was terrific, too, as a priest trying to make the terrorist do the right thing. Mickey also praised the performance of Sammi Davis, who played his love interest, but still felt she was too young to do love scenes with him because, although she was twenty-two at the time, she looked creepily younger.

When he saw the final cut of the movie, Mickey's world imploded. He had set out to make a sensitive portrayal of the situation in Northern Ireland but felt the film had been turned into a standard sex and shoot-'em-up thriller.

A Prayer for the Dying, directed by crime film veteran Mike Hodges, quickly died at the box office, but the controversy surrounding the subject matter and the star would rage on for a long time. Mickey fell into a depression for months afterwards at the way he felt his vision for the movie had been betrayed and he lost trust in people.

Mickey needed a lot of persuading to take on his next role as an alcoholic in *Barfly* (1987), especially as so many of his relatives had died from the demon drink. His father, grandfather, great-grandfather and uncles all perished after booze problems. So the last thing he wanted to do was glorify a drunk on screen. But he was in a dark place mentally at the time and the darkness of the script appealed to him.

Barfly was based on the life of hard-drinking writer and poet Charles Bukowski, who wrote the screenplay. Mickey played the very similar Henry Chinaski, a drunk who cruises seedy Los Angeles bars in an alcoholic haze and seems to enjoy getting beaten up frequently in bar brawls. But when a literary editor recognizes his writing talent, Henry's freewheeling lifestyle is suddenly threatened.

Mickey had never heard of Bukowski before filming, but read a couple of his books, met the writer as preparation, and got to like him – as did his brother Joey who became a drinking partner of the writer. Bukowski was a real character on set, drinking beer from early in the morning and trying to persuade Mickey to have one. But even though he was playing an alcoholic, Mickey stuck to ginseng, vitamins, and protein shakes during filming of the movie.

He also enjoyed working with colorful co-star Faye Dunaway – who would often be on the phone with her shrink for an hour before filming her first scene of the day – but Mickey didn't think much of the movie's director, Barbet Schroeder, whom he has since called "a prick", "a baby" and an "asshole."

Schroeder certainly went to extremes in order to get the movie made. The company which had been developing the film, Cannon, was all set to cancel it for financial reasons until the eccentric director showed up at the office of their president Menahem Golan with an electric saw. He threatened to cut his own finger off there and then if the movie wasn't given an immediate go ahead. To show he was serious, he pulled out a syringe of the painkiller Novocain and injected it into his little finger. He then said he would continue cutting off parts of his body until *Barfly* got the green light. Golan told him to go to hell. Then Schroeder turned on the saw. Whether it was a bluff or not, it worked, and *Barfly* went into production soon afterwards.

Mickey created one of his iconic characters in this film and few who saw it would forget the image of him shuffling down the more tattered streets of LA, sloppily dressed, unshaven and out of it.

A couple of years after the movie came out, Charles Bukowski wrote a novel called *Hollywood* which was a fictional account of his experiences during the production of *Barfly* and it is clear to see who might have been the inspiration for the character of Jack Bledsoe, the eccentric lead actor who is surrounded by an entourage of street urchins and pseudo gangsters.

Mickey would continue to be associated with Bukowski even up to the writer's death. In its obituary of the poet in 1994, the *New York Post* used a photo of Mickey as Henry Chinaski in the film instead of a picture of Bukowski.

Barfly was a positive experience for Mickey overall and made him feel a bit better about the world after losing his way following *A Prayer for the Dying*. His spirits were about to be lifted even further when he got the go-ahead to star in a movie he had long dreamed of making. *Homeboy* (1988) was a true passion project for Mickey, who wrote the script under the pen name of Eddie Cook. The name had a history. It was the false name he had once given to the cops after stealing some chocolate when he was a kid. Years later, it was still a name he was happy to hide his true identity behind.

The story of a brain-damaged boxer drifting from fight to fight long after he should have retired from the sport, *Homeboy* was inspired by the path Mickey may have taken in life if he hadn't stepped away from boxing when he did.

It saw his character, soft-spoken cowboy Johnny Walker – based on a troubled fighter who used to box in the same Miami gym as Mickey all those years ago – risking his life in the ring for one last shot at big winnings. His unscrupulous manager, Wesley Pendergass, who hides the extent of his medical condition from him, is played by Christopher Walken. The slow-paced film comes alive when they are on screen together, especially in the scene where Wesley tells the fighter his theory about why dinosaurs became extinct. That scene had its beginnings nine years earlier when Mickey and Christopher were having dinner at the Outlaw Inn in Kalispell, Montana, after a day's filming on *Heaven's Gate*. Walken outlined his theory about what happened to the dinosaurs – that they grew wings and flew away to another planet. That conversation with one of his idols stayed in Mickey's mind and when he wrote *Homeboy* and cast Walken in the film, he deliberately gave Christopher's character a bizarre speech about dinosaurs turning into birds.

Mickey's love interest in the film, Ruby, was played by his wife, Debra Feuer, from whom he was estranged at the time. Their characters share a sweet, tender, and ultimately doomed romance, but Mickey and Debra display a curious lack of chemistry on screen. Mickey had written the role with Feuer in mind and the pair had a good working relationship, despite the fact that their marriage was nearing its end.

As close as he was to the material, Mickey chose not to direct *Homeboy*. It was originally his intention to do so, and he spent a couple of weekends shooting some test footage. But when Mickey saw it, he realized he wasn't technically knowledgeable enough to create the look he wanted. So he brought in *Angel Heart*'s cinematographer Michael Seresin to direct the movie and he gave the film a terrific look, although the first-time director wasn't quite as successful with the pacing: the story drags in places.

Homeboy features cameos from some of boxing's most beloved figures, including ring announcer Michael Buffer, legendary trainer Bobby Slayton and ex-champ Iran Barkley. The film's memorable music was written and performed by Eric Clapton.

While *Homeboy* wasn't a commercial hit, the movie certainly has its moments and everyone involved could be proud of their efforts. Mickey followed it with another low-budget independent film, but one that offered a very different role from any the fans had seen before or since – and a performance of which he was very proud.

Francesco (1989) saw him play St Francis of Assisi. Given his off-screen reputation as something of a sinner, it was a surprise to see Mickey play a saint. But that was largely what had drawn him to the project in the first place. Mickey had been raised in the Catholic faith and is still a regular churchgoer who says his prayers every day. Some of his earliest memories are of going to church with his father and eating doughnuts and drinking milk with him afterwards. When his mother broke up with her husband and moved away to Miami with the kids, she joined the Episcopal Church and took Mickey along. But when he was seventeen and facing an uncertain future, Mickey decided to switch back to Catholicism and has stuck with his faith ever since.

He knew about several saints but wasn't too familiar with St Francis until he read up on him as research for *Francesco*. When he learned Francis had been a pampered playboy who lived life in the fast lane, Mickey knew this was a part to which he could relate.

He does a good job in the film portraying the switch to an entirely different life as Francis finds God then dedicates his life to helping the poor. That was partly thanks to director Liliana Cavani having the right combination of patience and faith to get the best out of Mickey. One scene called for him, as Francis, to stand on a mountain top willing God to speak to him and then suffering an emotional breakdown when it doesn't happen. Method actor Mickey just couldn't get into the right mood emotionally, even after nearly two hours of working up to it and, with time being money on a film set, some members of the crew started to look at their watches wondering when he would ever be ready to film a take. But Liliana came over and told him, "Forget about the time, fuck the time, you take all the time you want." Mickey was grateful and went back to his preparation. As he had the line, "Oh Father..." he started to think about his own father and that familiar picture of his dad in the bodybuilding pose. He looked to the skies thinking about how much he wished his own father would appear from the heavens and speak to him. That made Mickey ready to shoot the scene and he nailed a perfect take.

He had so much faith in Cavani that he later agreed to her request to shoot an extra scene for the film where he rolls around naked in the snow to cleanse himself symbolically of his sins – something he might not have done for other directors. He was less pleased about his decision when he found a paparazzi photographer had sneaked onto the set and later sold pictures of the naked cleansing to a magazine.

While his performance in Francesco is suitably serene, the low-budget film is somewhat let down by Mickey having a late 1980s haircut. It also seems odd that while the rest of the cast deliver their lines in English accents, Mickey uses his own speaking voice.

Director Liliana Cavani's decision to dramatize a series of incidents from the saint's life, rather than structure the film with a coherent narrative, doesn't make for easy viewing and the movie was little seen and quickly forgotten. Not that a movie about a saint finding God was ever going to be as big a hit as something with sex, violence, and explosions.

After making back-to-back independent films for comparatively little pay, Mickey welcomed a return to big-budget studio pictures, not least because the seven-figure salary would help out with his expensive tastes. But he was careful to pick out a fascinating character to play and chose well with *Johnny Handsome* (1989), an underrated revenge thriller which saw him cast as a most unusual criminal and wearing heavy prosthetic make-up for the opening scenes.

In a role originally intended for Al Pacino, who dropped out because he was not satisfied with the script, Mickey played career criminal John Sedley who has a severely disfigured face until kind-hearted prison surgeon Dr. Steven Fisher, played by Forest Whitaker, operates on him and gives the convict a handsome new appearance. When he leaves prison with a chance for a new life, Johnny just wants to get back at the double-crossing crooks who left him to be arrested and locked up, so he uses his new identity to lure them to their doom. Director Walter Hill cranks up the excitement, Morgan Freeman is terrific as a cynical cop, and Mickey brings power and pathos to his character's journey.

But although his performance was excellent, acting had lost its excitement for Mickey. It was becoming a boring, unfulfilling job for him. And when *Johnny Handsome* bombed at the box office, it was another disappointing setback.

His next movie, *Wild Orchid* (1990) was pretty awful but proved a happy experience for Mickey as he fell head-over-heels in love with his co-star, mouthwatering model Carré Otis. She played young lawyer Emily Reed who travels to sultry Rio de Janeiro on business and meets Mickey's character, mysterious and seductive millionaire businessman James Wheeler, who exposes her to a world of steamy perversions and various sexual shenanigans. It was a kind of low-rent *9½ Weeks* and was directed, and co-written, by that film's co-writer, soft-core king Zalman King.

In the film, Mickey gets to looks moody, wear nice clothes, ride his Harley Davidson, and deliver some dreadful dialogue during a performance which would see him nominated as Worst Actor at that year's Golden Raspberry Awards for the biggest disasters in cinema. There was a far from convincing performance from Otis whose well-educated character supposedly speaks six languages, but Carré even struggles with her native English. She looks good, though, which is perhaps more important in this kind of film.

The movie is most remembered for its passion-packed, climactic nude sex scene where Mickey and Carré were rumored to have had sex for real. The "did they or didn't they?" intrigue was good PR and perhaps helped *Wild Orchid* to avoid utter embarrassment at the box office and escape with moderate takings.

Much better entertainment was provided by Mickey's next cinematic outing, crime thriller *Desperate Hours* (1990). The movie was a remake of a 1955 film of the same title and saw Mickey in the lead role originally played by Humphrey Bogart. His character, Michael Bosworth, is an escaped con on the run from the law who hides out in a married couple's suburban home and proceeds to terrorize the family. Anthony Hopkins is excellent, as usual, as the head of the family and his scenes with Mickey really crackle. The film gave Mickey the opportunity to work again with one of his favorite directors, Michael Cimino, but – as with their previous efforts together – this one flopped, too.

Next came the leading candidate for worst movie of Mickey's career, the embarrassment that was *Harley Davidson and the Marlboro Man* (1991). Ironically, it saw him earn the biggest salary of his career – $2.6 million – thanks to some ace negotiating by his then agent, Rick Nicita of CAA. Mickey knew that the material was bad, but the fee was very attractive – especially as he had to pay for his big house, big cars, and big entourage.

There's no shame in taking roles in rubbish films just for the large salary. Bigger stars than Mickey Rourke have been there and done that. Whenever Michael Caine would get a bad review, he would tell the press, "OK, the movie was terrible, but the house I bought for my mother is beautiful."

But Mickey hated himself for taking the movie purely for the money and quickly fell out of love with the movie business altogether. It's no wonder, given the weak plotting and mindless violence of a film that sees his character, Harley Davidson (like the bike he rides), team up with smoking cowboy pal, Marlboro Man, played by a lousy Don Johnson, and turn to crime so they can raise money to save their favorite bar from closing. In between shootouts and fight scenes, the stars are saddled with dialogue so bad it made *Scooby Doo* look like Shakespeare.

Audiences quite rightly ignored the movie, directed by Simon Wincer, and while Mickey made a lot of money from the picture he lost all respect for himself. He decided the only way he could win it back was in the boxing ring and made the startling decision at this time to become a professional fighter. The former amateur boxer had long wanted to get back into the fight game and knew he would be too old if he waited any longer.

But before he could put on the gloves, Mickey had one last contractual obligation to Hollywood, crime thriller *White Sands* (1992). Starting with the discovery in the desert of a suitcase full of cash next to a man's dead body, the story twists and turns its way into a fairly standard thriller which gets a burst of energy whenever Mickey is on screen giving his intense performance as the shady and sinister Gorman Lennox. He was surrounded by good talent in this one, such as director Roger Donaldson and co-star Samuel L. Jackson, but Mickey just wasn't motivated by acting in movies any more.

His future, at least in the short term, was going to be all about boxing. And Mickey couldn't wait to get back in the ring.

3

LORD OF THE RING

Mickey Rourke nervously paced the dressing room at the War Memorial Auditorium in Fort Lauderdale, Florida, as he prepared to make his professional boxing debut. It was 23 May 1991 and he was about to face journeyman fighter and part-time car mechanic Steve Powell in a four-round contest. There would be no second take if he screwed up here. Playing make-believe in movies was over. This was all too real.

Adding to Mickey's anxiety was the fact that he had suffered a hand injury before the bout. He didn't want to cancel and upset both the promoters and the public, so he decided to suck it up, fight on, and go for it.

A packed house of 2,300 fans, curious to see if the Hollywood actor – who arrived at the venue in a white limousine – could really cut it in the boxing ring, were first treated to other fights involving the likes of fighting physician Dr. Harold "Hackie" Reitman and world cruiserweight champ Phil "Enforcer" Jackson.

Then, finally, it was the main event of the evening and Mickey, weighing in at 178 lbs, emerged ready to do battle, wearing gold satin shorts emblazoned with green shamrocks.

He was applauded to the ring by an audience relieved that he hadn't done what many suspected he might – lose his nerve and chicken out of the contest.

What followed was a scrappy, stop-start fight with Mickey starting out tentatively but gradually getting into his stride and making up in enthusiasm what he lacked in finesse. Restricted by his injury, he fought dirty with a few nasty tricks picked up in various boxing gyms down the years.

"Sometimes you do what you have to do," he told me when we discussed that first fight. It worked for him and he won the fight on the judges' decision.

The crowd, many of whom were Vietnam veterans, wasn't wildly impressed with his showboating, dancing around the ring, street brawl punches and dirty tactics. Some were booing and others were chanting "Mic-key sucks," but Mickey loved every minute.

Originally, Mickey had planned to have only one professional boxing match, but following the debut victory, the sport was back in his blood and it became the main focus of his life.

His ambition rapidly grew to win a title. He didn't get that but he did get self-respect – along with a succession of severe facial injuries.

* * *

It was on the set of his boxing movie, *Homeboy*, that Mickey first got the idea to return to the ring as a professional fighter. The climactic fight sequence wasn't working out as choreographed – everything looked clumsy and fake. So the star decided to throw away the script and improvise his own moves by boxing his equally enthusiastic opponent, an actual fighter, for real to add authenticity to the film's ending. Suddenly, all the excitement of those amateur fights came rushing back to him and, as he threw and took actual punches, he felt gloriously alive.

Looking back, Mickey feels he should have made the switch to pro boxing there and then. Instead, he stayed in acting for another three years. But film work wasn't making him happy. He longed for the unscripted adrenalin rush of boxing that would make him feel good about himself again. After all, when the bell rings, you can't say, "I'm not emotionally ready," or ask for more make-up – it's raw, rough and real, man against man, with no Hollywood bullshit.

When 1991 rolled around, Mickey realized he wasn't getting any younger and it would have to be now or never. To see if he still had fight skills, he went back to Miami's Fifth Street Gym for the first time in many years and sparred with various boxers there. He loved it, felt totally at home, and found he hadn't lost his ring ability. That's when he took the decision which stunned Hollywood – to swap films for fights. He then persuaded respected boxing insider Tommy Torino to manage him and fix him up with a professional fight.

The switch to boxing was more about self-respect than stardom and Mickey chose not to fight under his famous name. Instead, he hoped to enter the ring as Romeo Florentino, which sounded like a good fighter's name to him. But the promoters of his contests wouldn't hear of it. They were paying good money for Mickey Rourke, and therefore they wanted his recognizable – and bankable – name on the posters.

So he settled on adding a middle name: "Marielito." It was a

Cuban nickname and he chose it as a mark of respect to the tough Cuban kids he had grown up with, and fought with, in Miami. *Marielito* was a term applied to the 125,000 Cuban boat people who fled to the US in 1980 as part of an exodus of refugees from the Cuban port of Mariel. Al Pacino's title character in the 1983 movie *Scarface* was a fictional Marielito.

Mickey "Marielito" Rourke fought eight professional bouts in arenas around the world, ranging from Argentina to the Bahamas, Germany to Japan. Many of the audiences came out of curiosity and even a desire to see the Hollywood star beaten up, but Mickey held his own, won their respect, and emerged with an unbeaten record. Despite the fact that he was a pretty lazy trainer much of the time. Not for him the fighter's discipline of getting up at six every morning and going for a long run. He was more inclined to do a bit of gym work, then have a rest, hit the punching bag, and then have a cigarette.

But things gradually improved under the guidance of the leading fight trainer he hired to knock him into shape and make him a winner. Freddie Roach, a former boxer himself, knew what he was talking about and is today widely considered the best in the business as trainer to the likes of Manny Pacquiao and Amir Khan. Roach took a no-nonsense approach with Mickey and even quit in despair early in their association when the actor-turned-boxer stayed out all night partying when he was supposed to be resting and training. "I don't train fighters to lose," were his parting words.

He had shown up in the gym on seven straight days to train Mickey, but Rourke showed up on only one of those days. Roach ripped into the star for his lack of commitment and reduced Mickey to tears with his angry tirade. The actor's plea for him to stay fell on deaf ears.

But Mickey phoned Freddie every day for the next thirty days begging him to come back and promising to do better. He kept telling Roach how much the fight game meant to him and insisted he was ready to get serious. Roach relented and returned to train Rourke on the condition Mickey gave him 110 per cent – and that's just what he got.

Mickey knuckled down to his training, got a sense of discipline for the first time in his life, dropped his fighting weight down from 210 to 168 lbs and eventually found greater reserves of stamina and skill, which got him through his super-middleweight fights.

Freddie's motivational magic between rounds also helped. With Mickey slumped on the stool and having a hard time, the trainer would say things like: "Do you want to go back to acting? No? Well go back in there and knock this guy out."

In the gym, Rourke sparred with, and got beaten around by, up-and-coming fighter James "Lights Out" Tony, who would later go on to beat the great Evander Holyfield. Tony managed to break his cheekbone, even though Mickey had a head guard on when they sparred. But those sessions toughened up Mickey and improved his ring craft.

His results and performances became impressive – he scored a first-round knockout over Darrell Miller in Japan, KO'ed Thomas McCoy in three rounds in Germany, and did the same in Spain to Terry "The Hook" Jesmer.

Other celebrities have switched to short-lived sports careers with varying levels of success – from British glamour model Jordan taking up dressage and polo to Hollywood actress Geena Davis narrowly missing out on a place in the US archery team for the Sydney Olympics. But none had the run of consistently good results that Mickey had – except for the late acting legend Paul Newman who won several times as a race car driver, finished second in the Le Mans 24 Hour Race, and entered the *Guinness Book of Records* as the oldest driver ever to win a professional motor race when he won the Daytona 24 Hours at the age of seventy.

Mickey loved his time boxing professionally, particularly for the mixture of electricity and fear he felt each time he was about to enter the ring. It was therapeutic for him after all the recent pain and frustration in his life. After all those years of scripted movies and several takes, he now had the strange thrill of not knowing what was going to happen next. When the bell sounded, it was like the moment a film camera's red light went on and he knew he had to deliver.

He also brought showbiz panache to the sport – entering to Guns 'n' Roses hit "Sweet Child o' Mine" and sometimes fighting in multi-colored shorts designed by Gianni Versace. Hollywood pals would show up at his fights and *Pope of Greenwich Village* co-star Eric Roberts was among his most enthusiastic supporters.

Mickey shook up a sport that was running short of charismatic figures at that time and even made it onto the cover of prestigious magazine *World Boxing* in June 1994.

Mickey the boxer became a box-office draw and, despite getting only $250 for his first pro fight, eventually earned more than $1 million from his boxing career. He wanted to supplement his income – and expensive lifestyle – with the occasional film role, but that proved tricky because he couldn't get an insurance bond. In other words, because he was fighting at the same time, the risk was too great and companies were extremely reluctant to insure a film with him in it.

But he was happy enough traveling the globe as a pro fighter. Hollywood came back to him when red-hot director Quentin Tarantino, a huge Mickey Rourke fan, offered Mickey a key role in *Pulp Fiction* as Butch Coolidge, a veteran boxer bribed by a mobster to throw his latest fight. It was a great role, perfect for Mickey, and could have catapulted him right back to the movie big time, but he didn't even read the script. He was preparing for a fight in Kansas against Tom Bentley at the time and didn't want to be distracted. After Mickey passed on the part, action star Bruce Willis got the role of Butch instead. He did a good job but surely the acclaimed movie would have been even more authentic and entertaining with Mickey in the role.

Mickey knows now that passing on *Pulp Fiction* was a mistake but he had no regrets at the time – especially after he KO'ed Bentley in the first round. He was getting a bigger rush from fighting than he had ever experienced in films. The crowds gradually warmed to him as well. As fight fans saw he was serious about the sport, they gave him their respect.

It was a little harder to win over the sportswriters. Newspaper reports from his fight career carried headlines like "ROURKE'S LATEST FIGHT NOTHING BUT A FARCE" and "FANS BOO ROURKE AFTER DRAW." Some of the press in Miami thought he was the biggest fake tough guy to come out of Florida since Vanilla Ice. But the fans nevertheless turned out in big numbers to watch Mickey fight. He had crowds of 10,000 and 15,000 at some of his contests.

Not all of the fans were supportive however. When he went to Hamburg, Germany, to fight Thomas McCoy, audience members pelted him with bottles in the ring. Rourke encouraged the frenzied crowd to keep on throwing the bottles until Freddie Roach urged him to stop winding up the fight goers in case things got out of hand and they got killed.

Mickey got a much warmer welcome when fighting in Japan, where he was as famous for his TV commercials as for his movies. Mickey had shot big-money Asian market–only ads for Suntory whisky and Daihatsu cars. Mickey admires Japanese culture and once bought a Samurai sword in Tokyo. To this day, some of his most frenzied fans are the Japanese.

Sadly, they didn't see much of him in the ring because his fight in the Tokyo Dome was over in just two minutes with his opponent Darrell "Big Chief" Miller decked by a bizarre punch, more of a fly-swatting move than a champion's blow, but effective nevertheless. It was just as well he finished that fight early as Marielito was sick with the flu that night and knew he wouldn't be able to last more than two rounds.

On a trip to Argentina, he got to meet one of his boxing heroes, Carlos Monzon. The legendary fighter was serving a prison sentence for killing his common-law wife. Mickey visited him in his Argentinean jail and even sparred a little with him in there.

Mickey was gradually being accepted and even embraced by the fight community in America and befriended legendary fighters like Evander Holyfield and Sugar Ray Leonard. As time went on, the actor-turned-fighter felt more comfortable in the company of sportsmen than of movie people.

At one point in his boxing career, he turned to the biggest legend of them all for help. Mickey was so nervous about an upcoming fight in which he feared he was outmatched that he couldn't sleep at night and instead just lay in bed shaking and sweating. He decided to turn for advice to his old inspiration, Muhammad Ali. Mickey called up the champ's friend and official photographer Howard Bingham and asked him for the favor of getting Ali to call him in a bid to settle his nerves.

The next night, Ali came on the phone. He didn't remember Mickey from the Fifth Street Gym days in Miami but he understood what he was going through and spent almost twenty minutes on the phone to Mickey, calming him down and boosting his confidence. As a result, Mickey was fine in the fight.

Ali's health deteriorated in the later stages of his career, not so much because of the fights but as a legacy of all the sparring he had done in training for them. Mickey had the same problem. During his pro career, Mickey was sparring up to thirty rounds a week, not always wearing head guards, which made him claustrophobic.

One of those sparring sessions was with boxing great Thomas Hearns and Mickey came to realize how that champion had earned the nickname "Hit Man." Hearns hit Mickey so hard that he suffered delayed concussion, feeling it ten hours afterwards, at midnight. Mickey suddenly felt so sick that he tried to phone for a doctor, but his head was so messed up he couldn't make his fingers touch the number keys.

As his own fighting career wound down, Mickey began to experience symptoms of brain damage, being unable to remember what he had done the night before. In addition to short-term memory loss, he was experiencing problems with his balance. Frightened of suffering permanent brain damage – and disintegrating like the boxer he played in *Homeboy* – Mickey arranged to take a neurological exam. He failed it. And the doctor insisted, "You should stop fighting immediately."

Punch-drunk Mickey begged him to let him carry on, saying he had three more fights scheduled and the third one would have been for a WBO championship belt – a prize that would have meant more to him than an Oscar. He told the neurologist, "I just need to fight three more times."

But the expert replied, "Listen, you can't even get hit in the head one more time, your neuro is so bad."

When Mickey revealed how much he would be earning for his next fight, the surgeon replied, "You won't be able to count it."

Faced with the choice of quitting the ring or risking becoming a drooling vegetable, Marielito made the wise decision and threw in the towel.

His last fight, in 1994, was a draw with "Irish" Sean Gibbons in Davie, Florida. After six wins and two draws, Mickey retired from the ring unbeaten but had sustained several injuries over the previous three years, including broken bones in each hand, broken ribs, and a few concussions. Mickey had also sustained facial injuries which required several operations. These ranged from a split tongue to a compressed cheekbone. He ended up with far fewer teeth in his mouth and his nose was repeatedly broken. Mickey needed five operations on his nose, which was rebuilt with cartilage taken from his ear.

Mickey's face was reconstructed by a cosmetic surgeon used by other boxers and nicknamed "The Butcher." During one of the procedures, The Butcher stuck a long needle into Mickey's lip and pulled out an infection. His botched work left Mickey's lip sticking out a long way. He was supposed to go back for one more corrective session with The Butcher, but he couldn't face the pain and never returned. It would take four years for his face to return to relative normality.

So Mickey emerged from the boxing years with a freakish appearance far different from his pretty-boy looks of the past. He had suffered the biggest facial collapse since those melting Nazis at the end of *Raiders of the Lost Ark*.

He looks better now but the legacy of those boxing batterings will be with him forever.

The nerve damage in his hands means he is unable to do anything intricate with them and they still shake from time to time. Boxing also had an effect on his walking, which was noticed when he kept tripping on his way to the stage at late-2008 and early-2009 awards shows. He sometimes likes to go surfing but is lousy at it because his balance is so bad.

Boxing had given Mickey a discipline and a routine that his acting career had lacked, and he knew he could take those tools with him into his future film work. But the sport had also messed up his looks and resuming his movie career at the top level would not be as easy as he thought.

In fact, trying to make his way back to movie stardom would prove Mickey's toughest fight of all.

Mickey "Marielito" Rourke's Professional Boxing Record

6 Wins (4 knockouts, 2 decisions), 0 Losses, 2 Draws

Res.	Record	Opponent	Type	Rd., Time	Date	Location	Notes
Draw	6-0-2	Sean Gibbons	Majority draw	4	September 8, 1994	Davie, Florida, USA	Scoring was 37-39 for Gibbons, 38-38 and 38-38
Win	6-0-1	Thomas McCoy	TKO	3 (4)	November 20, 1993	Hamburg, Germany	
Win	5-0-1	Bubba Stotts	TKO	3 (4)	July 24, 1993	Joplin, Missouri, USA	
Win	4-0-1	Tom Bentley	KO	1 (4)	March 30, 1993	Kansas City, Missouri, USA	
Win	3-0-1	Terry Jesmer	Decision	4	December 12, 1992	Oviedo, Spain	
Win	2-0-1	Darrell Miller	KO	1 (4) 2:14	June 23, 1991	Tokyo, Japan	
Draw	1-0-1	Francisco Harris	Majority draw	4	April 25, 1992	Miami Beach, Florida, USA	Scoring was 38-39 for Harris, 38-38 and 38-38
Win	1-0	Steve Powell	Unanimous decision	4	May 23, 1991	Fort Lauderdale, Florida, USA	Scoring was 38-37, 38-37 and 39-37

87

4
A Life on Screen – Part II

"What you need for this role is a Mickey Rourke type," the Hollywood studio executive told Francis Ford Coppola.

The legendary director was discussing the casting of a key character in his new movie, *The Rainmaker*, with bosses from Paramount, the studio for which he had made *The Godfather* twenty-five years earlier. A little confused by the "Rourke type" comment, Coppola said, "But Mickey is still out there, still working… why not just get him?"

The room fell silent. The Paramount people looked at each other uncomfortably. Mickey was trouble, wasn't he? A hell-raising head case. Was he really still working? Certainly his recent roles, ranging from a gay bank robber to a flamboyant psychiatrist, were in films barely seen by anyone.

What Mickey needed was someone with authority and talent to give him another shot at the big time – and Coppola, who had directed him in *Rumble Fish* and had long championed the actor, was prepared to be that person. Ignoring the skeptics in the room, he insisted Mickey was the right man for the role. And Mickey responded with a great performance in *The Rainmaker*. That was the first step in a long and winding road back to the top.

* * *

Mickey didn't entirely abandon acting during his boxing years. He made three films in that period – all of which were set around bank robberies. The first was a TV movie for cable channel HBO called *The Last Outlaw* (1993). It was a western, set in 1880, shot in Santa Fe, New Mexico, and saw Mickey riding a horse while wearing a ten-gallon hat, chaps, and spurs, and toting guns.

He played the lead role of Graff, head of a ruthless gang of former Confederate soldiers who rob banks and kill anyone who gets in their way. When the gang betrays him, Graff sets out to hunt down each of his treacherous enemies and violently kills them one by one. It was directed by Geoff Murphy who had previous experience in westerns, having been behind the camera on *Young Guns 2*. But this one was let down by its slow pace and never came close to the superior quality of other productions on HBO, the channel behind *The Sopranos*, *Band of Brothers*, *Sex and the City*, and a string of award-winning TV movies. It was fun, though, to see Mickey playing a nineteenth-century renegade.

Next came *F.T.W.* (1994) also known as *The Last Ride*, a downbeat movie, co-written by Mickey under his now grander pen name of "Sir" Eddie Cook – who, in an inside joke, had apparently been knighted since writing *Homeboy*. In the film he plays rodeo rider Frank T. Wells – the initials of the title, which was also supposed to stand for "Fuck The World" – who has just been released from prison after serving a term for manslaughter and is trying to get back into the old routine when he meets and falls for Scarlett Stuart, played by Lori Singer, an emotionally disturbed, beautiful bank robber on the run who changes his life – but not necessarily for the better. Although Mickey was thrilled to see his second script produced, it was a blow when *F.T.W.* failed to make it onto movie screens and went straight to video.

Fall Time (1995) found him playing a gay bank robber named Florence. Seriously! This surreal crime film, set in 1950s America, starts with Florence declaring his love for his partner in crime and life, played by Stephen Baldwin, and by the end of the movie both characters will be dead. The gay storyline isn't really developed in the form of any love scenes – this is no *Brokeback Bank Job* – as the homosexuality takes second place to the heist. In the end, it's just a strange little shoot-'em-up featuring some more outlaw posturing from Mickey. It was not the kind of film ever likely to return Mickey to the big time.

When he hung up his boxing gloves, Mickey knew he had the talent to be an acting champion again but just wanted the opportunity to show his skills alongside the big names of the time. He said back then, "You put me in something with Alec Baldwin or Daniel Day-Lewis or Kevin Costner and I'll eat their assholes."

Instead of that award-winning trio of actors, his next few co-stars included Jean-Claude Van Damme, Tupac Shakur and, once again, Carré Otis. *Exit in Red* (1996) marked the uneagerly awaited reteaming of Mickey and Carré Otis on screen for the first time since *Wild Orchid*. He plays a psychiatrist and she co-stars as the lawyer who loves him, but there are few sexual sparks between them this time, not least because Mickey's character is more attracted to a femme fatale, played by B-movie actress Annabel Schofield, who ends up framing him for murder. Because he has a checkered past himself, the shrink struggles to convince the authorities he is innocent and has to take matters into his own hands. The movie is silly throughout, and Mickey fails to convince as an experienced psychiatrist, sporting long blond hair, foppish clothes, and sunglasses, and smoking through a long cigarette holder.

He had a much harder look in his next film, a gritty and violent crime drama shot and set on the mean streets of Brooklyn, called *Bullet* (1996). It was co-written by Mickey, again under the name of Sir Eddie Cook, with Bruce Rubenstein, whose family background inspired the story. Mickey also served as music supervisor on *Bullet*, overseeing a varied soundtrack that veered from Vivaldi to Right Said Fred, and Barry White to hip-hop. His boxing trainer, Freddie Roach, was hired as fight coordinator for the film.

Mickey took the lead role of self-destructive heroin addict Butch "Bullet" Stein who gets out of prison and straight back into trouble, robbing junkies and stabbing a drug dealer in the eye. Mickey's friend John Eons III plays his best mate in the movie, and future Oscar winner Adrien Brody is the sensitive and artistic little brother whom Bullet is desperate to protect at all costs.

But the most noteworthy co-star was rapper Tupac Shakur, playing feared local drug lord Tank, who fights a street war with Bullet and shoots him dead at the end after uttering the cool line, "The music's over, motherfucker."

Tupac and Mickey bonded well during filming and found lots in common, both of them being perceived as bad boys but possessing the souls of poets. However, their friendship was not to last long. In September 1996, after seeing a Mike Tyson fight in Las Vegas, Tupac was the victim of a drive-by shooting. He was struck in the chest, pelvis, right hand, and thigh, and died from his injuries several days later. The tragedy hit Mickey hard and the star still keeps a picture of his slain friend in his home.

Although *Bullet*, released a month after Shakur's death, didn't do much at the box office, it had an authentic feel about it and Mickey could be proud of the movie. It is hard to say the same about his next effort, though, the action flick *Double Team* (1997).

A mix of martial arts mayhem, massive explosions, poor plotting, and dismal dialogue, the movie was a bit of a joke but, to his credit, Mickey took it seriously and underwent rigorous martial arts training and strenuous bodybuilding to prepare for the fight scenes, many of them shirtless, required in his role as international terrorist Stavros. His co-stars were the "Muscles from Brussels" action star Jean-Claude Van Damme, as an anti-terrorist agent, and tattooed basketball bad boy turned reality TV star Dennis Rodman, playing a flamboyant arms dealer who inserts basketball jargon into most of his lame lines. Van Damme's character spends much of the movie trying to eliminate Mickey's and there's a fun showdown between them at the end in an ancient coliseum rigged with land mines. The flop film's cheesiest but most gloriously entertaining moment comes when Mickey Rourke sends a man-eating tiger against Jean-Claude Van Damme and the pocket dynamo from Brussels defends himself by kicking the charging beast.

It must have seemed like a good idea at the time to make *Another 9½ Weeks* (1997). Mickey needed a hit, and a sequel to

93

his biggest ever box-office success would seem to fit the bill. But Kim Basinger wasn't going to return. She had bigger fish to fry, having just filmed her Oscar-winning role in *LA Confidential*. So the absence of her character, Elizabeth, would have to be dealt with in the script. Set ten years after the original, the sequel sees Mickey's character, John Gray, pining for his lost love and following her trail to Paris, only to find Elizabeth has died. But he gets over his disappointment by having a fling with her best friend, played by model Angie Everhart, who has read Elizabeth's diary and is ready and willing for some of the same sex play with John. He is soon covering her naked body in rose petals, red wine, and honey, but his heart isn't in it this time. The quality isn't there either, and this follow-up film doesn't come remotely close to the excitement, atmosphere, or eroticism of the original.

Just when it seemed Mickey's post-boxing acting comeback was going nowhere, Francis Ford Coppola suddenly called and offered him a potentially career-reviving role in his major new movie *The Rainmaker* (1997). Mickey knew studio chiefs had been hesitant but Coppola had fought to add him to a cast including much hotter names like Matt Damon, Clare Danes, and Danny DeVito. He wasn't going to let Coppola down.

Grateful for the opportunity and delighted to be working again with the director against whom he judges all others, Mickey gave a scene-stealing performance in the prestige project, which John Grisham would call the best screen adaptation of one of his books.

Sporting greased-back silver hair, a neat goatee beard, yellow-tinted sunglasses, and sharp suits, Mickey is fun to watch as

Bruiser Stone, a slick, shifty, and shrewd veteran lawyer who gives Matt Damon's law student character a job with his minor law firm, which leads to the rookie landing the case of a lifetime. Mickey was so entertaining that audiences who viewed the film at preview test screenings kept saying they wanted to see more of his character. So Coppola gave them their wish by calling Mickey back to shoot extra scenes that were edited into the final cut. Up to this point, Mickey had generally chosen not to attend premieres of his movies because, in common with other perfectionist actors, he doesn't like watching himself on screen. But he made an exception for this one and liked what he saw.

The Rainmaker made $50 million at the US box office, but being in a hit didn't give Mickey the kind of career boost he might have expected. Instead of offers from other major studios and leading directors, he was catapulted back to the world of low-budget and often lower-quality movies, starting with a small role in *Buffalo '66* (1998).

This bleak drama with a meager budget of $1.5 million was written and directed by Vincent Gallo, who also starred as a young man just out of prison who managed to hide the fact he was in jail from his dysfunctional parents who think instead that he got married and went to work far away. When he goes to visit them, he needs a woman to pretend to be his bride and kidnaps a tap dancer, played by Christina Ricci, whom he forces to play the part.

Mickey, in the role of a sleazy and vengeful bookie, called The Bookie, which took less than a day to film, is in the movie for only a few minutes but still manages to act everyone else off the screen. His character was owed $10,000 by Gallo's character over a losing bet on the Buffalo Bills in the Super Bowl. When he couldn't pay, The Bookie forced him to take the fall for one of his criminal cronies and serve the prison sentence.

The story of how he came to participate in the film is just as entertaining as anything in the movie. Mickey was struggling for cash at the time – owing money on back taxes among other things – and was finding it hard to get hired for movies. Vincent Gallo understood the situation and had a neat solution, offering to pay Mickey $100,000 in cash to be in *Buffalo '66*. Mickey got straight on a plane to Buffalo, New York, did his work for four hours, and left with a paper bag full of money.

American movie stars generally don't like to take on TV work, believing it is a step down and lowers their mystique, but beggars can't be choosers and hard-up Mickey took on the lead part in a US cable TV film called *Thicker Than Blood* (1998), both for the money and the welcome opportunity to play a nice-guy role. He gives a good, sensitive performance as Father Frank Larkin, a Catholic priest trying to help troubled street kids in his parish. Given his Catholic background, Mickey looked comfortable in the role and elevated the material with some underplayed acting.

Next came another brief but flashy performance in crime thriller *Thursday* (1998), a kind of *Pulp Fiction* wannabe in which Mickey shows up as a bad guy named Kasarov. He is one of a series of hoods who come calling after a former-drug-dealer-gone-straight, played by Thomas Jane, makes the mistake of allowing his heroin-dealer mate, played by Aaron Eckhart, to stay at his place for a few days. Despite the good cast and some interesting ideas, the film made no impact.

Then it was violence all the way in *Point Blank* (1998) which sees a busload of dangerous criminals take over a Texas shopping mall and shoot every shopper, security guard, or cop who comes anywhere near them. Into this mayhem wades Mickey's pumped-up character, Ruby Ray, who plans to rescue his escaped convict brother from the center of the carnage by going all *Die Hard* and fighting a one-man war against all comers. Former real-life jailbird and boxer Danny Trejo, who would later star with Mickey in both *Animal Factory* and *Once Upon a Time in Mexico*, is also fun to watch as the toughest of the bad guys, but otherwise the movie is just lots and lots of mindless butchery.

Suddenly, however, a passage from under-par B-movies to artistic epics opened up as Mickey got the kind of out-of-the-blue offer that great actors dream about. Reclusive but brilliant director Terrence Malick wanted him for a role in his long awaited World War II film *The Thin Red Line* (1998), which was to be the meticulous moviemaker's first picture in twenty years.

Every actor in Hollywood was keen to be part of this landmark project about the conflict in the South Pacific, and it was a great tribute to Mickey that he was selected as part of the large ensemble cast while bigger stars who had chased after roles, including Tom Cruise, Leonardo DiCaprio and Robert De Niro, did not.

So Mickey headed off to Australia for the filming with high hopes for his role as a battle-scarred soldier and was thrilled to be working with Malick, a cinematic craftsman who had won his respect with the 1975 classic *Badlands*.

But it was all to end in disappointment as Mickey's role was eventually spliced out of the final cut. He wasn't alone. The same thing happened to Gary Oldman, Viggo Mortensen and Billy Bob Thornton as the director edited down his five-hour cut to the contracted running time of under three hours.

Mickey does get thanked in the end credits but that was little consolation. He felt he gave one of his best ever performances in *The Thin Red Line* and yet no one got to see it. Meanwhile, the rambling film fared badly at the box office, yet became a favorite with critics and landed seven Oscar nominations, but no wins.

Short of money and good opportunities, and feeling like a has-been, Mickey now drifted from one low-budget film to another, making the kind of movies destined for the DVD discount bins rather than the big screen. These included the forgettable drama *Cousin Joey* (1999), produced by action star Steven Seagal and directed by fashion designer Sante D'Orazio, about a pair of drug addicts caught up in the New York underworld.

Shergar (1999) was inspired by the mystery disappearance of the great racehorse of the same name and imagined what might have happened to the Derby winner. Sightings of the movie have been as rare as glimpses of the stallion himself in recent years but it's worth tracking down as the film is actually quite involving and intriguing. Mickey plays Gavin O'Rourke, a member of an IRA terror cell that kidnaps the horse and holds him for ransom, only for a young stable boy to foil their plans.

Mickey's next effort, *Out in Fifty* (1999), also had its moments. Another low-budget crime drama, this one found Mickey as vengeful Jack Bracken, a pill-popping, hard-drinking cop hunting down the man who killed his wife. But, again, few people saw it.

Even fewer saw *Shades* (1999), an odd film that's now hard to find and not really worth the effort. A Belgian picture shot in Antwerp and Brussels, it stars Mickey as down-on-his-luck Hollywood film director Paul S. Sullivan who goes to Belgium and makes a movie over there for the money – a case of art imitating life perhaps? The movie within a movie shows the film business to be full of unscrupulous producers and prima donna stars, so they certainly got that part right.

Could it get any more bizarre for Mickey than a low-budget movie in Belgium? Unfortunately, the answer is yes. When Steve Buscemi called and offered Mickey the part of a transvestite in a prison movie he was directing, Mickey thought his old co-star from *The Last Outlaw* was joking. Surely he wanted him to play a standard tough guy convict. He realized Steve was serious only when the script for *Animal Factory* (2000) turned up in his mail box with a note asking him to look at the part of flamboyant jailbird Jan the Actress. Buscemi really rated Mickey as an actor and knew that role would require someone terrific to make it seem real rather than a joke. Mickey found himself intrigued by the idea of playing a character described as a muscular transvestite with green fingernails, thick lipstick, and a lisp. He saw it as a true acting challenge, and Mickey really committed to the role.

For the performance, he used his memories of his early days in LA working as a bouncer in the transvestite club. He had also worked in one in Miami when he was eighteen, so he knew the cursing, lisping, muscular tranny types and went all out to turn himself into one of them for the film. He had his dentist take out the fixed bridge that keeps his two fake front teeth in place and that helped him achieve the lisp. Next he went to a Beverly Hills nail salon for a French manicure and then had his eyebrows waxed and reshaped so they were higher and longer. He also had his hair cut extremely short.

Continuing his usual tradition of picking out his own outfits for roles, he went to famous adults-only LA shops like Trashy Lingerie and The Pleasure Chest and bought a red satin bra and red G-string to wear in the film. As he visited other lingerie stores and boutiques over the course of ten days, trying on women's clothes, Mickey would get strange looks, especially from customers and staff who recognized him. He even ended up in the tabloids as speculation grew about his strange shopping habits.

But Mickey shrugged it all off and got on with assembling his cross-dressing convict look, cutting the sleeves off an old blue cowboy-style shirt and tying it up at the waist, adding some hip-hugging jeans and powder-blue shoes with spiked heels and fur on the front. He completed the ensemble by having a belly ring put in – a piercing that hurt like hell. Then, to get into character, he flew on the plane from LA to Vancouver wearing his full outfit and make-up for the film.

The movie, adapted from his book by one of Steve Buscemi's *Reservoir Dogs* co-stars, ex-con Edward Bunker, sees Edward Furlong playing a first-time offender thrown into a prison with a bunch of freaks and tough guys including characters played by previous Mickey Rourke co-stars Willem Dafoe and Danny Trejo. Mickey's best moment in the film is a memorable monologue – which he wrote himself – where Jan talks about wanting to become a butterfly and flying beyond the prison bars, then all the way to Paris. The lines were inspired by Mickey reasoning that institutionalized characters like Jan would try to cope with their situation by living in their heads and indulging in just such delusional fantasies.

Mickey was rewarded for his efforts with some terrific reviews but there were to be no large audiences for the grim picture about prison life. With his career in trouble, Mickey was really low on cash and on the lookout for a role in a big-budget movie which could get him back on track. At that point a guardian angel walked across his path, in the rather unlikely form of Sylvester Stallone.

The Rocky and Rambo superstar was dining in an Italian restaurant, saw Mickey eating alone at a nearby table, free of the usual entourage that had surrounded him the past, and went over to offer him a job in his next movie, *Get Carter* (2000). Stallone told him, "Listen, I'm doing this movie and I need somebody in it who looks like they can kick my ass. You look like you can kick my ass."

Mickey, who could barely afford to pay for the bowl of spaghetti he was eating, eagerly accepted the job as villainous club owner Cyrus Paice in Sly's remake of the classic 1971 Michael Caine crime film. But when the contract came through, the money on offer was so startlingly low that Mickey found it disrespectful and turned the job down, but thanked Stallone anyway for the offer. That Mickey did end up in the film was all down to Stallone's generosity. When the producer couldn't or wouldn't pay Mickey what he felt he was worth, Sly doubled Mickey's salary by chipping in the extra money out of his own pocket.

But while the money was right in the end, the film wasn't. From Stallone's strange goatee beard to the jerky camera movements and underwhelming script, there was something not quite right about it. Stallone plays mob enforcer Jack Carter who sets out to find and kill those responsible for his brother's murder. But it's just not a patch on the rough, tough original, and Michael Caine's appearance in a cameo reminded viewers of that fact. Still, the *Get Carter* remake was a million times better than Mickey's next movie.

Hopefully, Mickey Rourke's fortunes will never again sink so low that he has to take a role in another crummy killer insect movie like *They Crawl* (2001). He appears in one scene as weirdo Tiny Frakes, trying to mislead a police detective that he knows nothing about a series of murders caused by a rampaging posse of genetically mutated cockroaches. The movie is so bad on every level that it leaves you wondering how films like this even get made.

Mickey's titanic career was sinking fast now. But then Sean Penn threw him a lifeline. Penn was directing the haunting, intense drama *The Pledge* (2001), starring Jack Nicholson as a veteran detective trying to solve the murder of a little girl, and hired some of the best actors around for cameo appearances, including Benicio Del Toro, Helen Mirren, Vanessa Redgrave... and Mickey Rourke. Sean and Mickey had been great friends during their early days in Hollywood but then had a falling out and hadn't spoken in over ten years. Penn broke the silence, called Mickey, asked him if he was short of cash, and when his old friend said he was, he asked Rourke to come and work for him on his new film. Mickey's role was that of James Olstad, the grieving and tormented father of another murdered child who now goes through the motions working as a janitor in a rest home. In his one scene, acting opposite Jack Nicholson, Mickey reminded Hollywood just what a powerful actor he was, getting every ounce of emotion out of his tale of loss.

Mickey was thrilled to be back acting alongside a real talent like Jack Nicholson, whom he thought was very generous and giving in the scene by taking a back seat and allowing him to shine. He worked for three months preparing for that one day's work – and it's an acting master class. The film doesn't follow the conventions of most psychological thrillers but is a thought provoking and well made piece of work.

It was back to lower-quality stuff for Mickey's next movie, *Picture Claire* (2001), a "wrong time, wrong place" thriller starring Juliette Lewis as a woman who is mistaken for a killer and ends up fleeing both the police and some vengeful drug dealers. Gina Gershon co-stars as the real murderer and Mickey is third in the credits, but doesn't hang around long, as her victim, Eddie, a toothpick-chewing, leather-jacket-wearing, foul-mouthed criminal. His only scene is set in a donut shop where Juliette Lewis, as Claire, asks him for directions. Eddie doesn't want to be bothered, spills coffee over her, tells her to fuck off, and calls her a cunt. While she is in the bathroom wiping coffee off her clothes, Eddie's lusty girlfriend, Lily, played by Gina Gershon, comes into the now empty donut shop, straddles her lover, and then strangles him with some wire before rushing out. The elderly store owner wrongly identifies Juliette's character as the killer and, confused, she goes on the run.

It's all fairly routine after that with the only other moment in the movie to watch out for being Tori Spelling's future husband Dean McDermott playing "attendant at station" – very badly.

There was one amusing moment during filming in Toronto, although the movie makers weren't laughing. They called for silence while shooting a street scene only for a woman to keep blowing a whistle, thereby ruining the takes. The phantom whistler was eventually arrested for causing a disturbance and taken away by the cops. But viewers can pretty much blow the whistle on this movie once Mickey's memorable scene is over.

Mickey had worked hard to banish his old hell raiser reputation and felt that his professionalism in recent movies like *The Pledge* and *Get Carter* could help him land the juicy roles he wanted in prestige projects. But he clearly hadn't done enough to impress some people, for Mickey lost out at this time on a lead role in the long-in-development erotic thriller *In the Cut* (2003) because Nicole Kidman, making her producing debut on the film and given final approval on all casting decisions, didn't want him in the movie. Mickey was frustrated, especially as Kidman had discounted him without ever meeting him.

Mickey needed someone to believe in him and help him towards the kind of opportunities his talent deserved. Enter his new agent – David Unger. Mickey didn't much like the script of the drug movie *Spun* (2002) and, with the exception of Eric Roberts, had little interest in the cast, but he made the movie anyway because his new agent told him to do so.

Mickey had put his career in the hands of the young man

who wanted to chart a new course for his client, handpicking supporting roles for Mickey in films by up-and-coming directors that Unger said would lead him back to the big time. *Spun* was one of these projects, and was directed by Jonas Åkerlund, who had shown a promising visual style as director of eye-catching pop videos like Madonna's "Ray of Light" and U2's "Beautiful Day."

David Unger first met Mickey Rourke, and a few of his dogs, in a coffee shop, and treated him with great respect. Unger admitted he was a young agent with a lot to prove, said he believed in Mickey, and asked Mickey to have the same belief in him. Some of his colleagues at ICM may have been skeptical, but Unger was confident he could bring about a comeback for his new client. Unger's grandfather was a movie producer, and the young agent was steeped in the movie business, having been brought up on films like *Rumble Fish, Diner,* and *9½ Weeks*. He knew if he targeted directors of his thirty-something generation, they would feel the same way.

So he lined up meetings with those directors. Mickey would meet them, apologize for his past deeds, and say he was ready to be reliable and become a movie star again. All these "getting to know you" meetings were of the kind any promising young actor trying to make his way in Hollywood goes through, but Mickey was doing them as he approached middle age.

The other things the new agent asked him to do to make himself more appealing to moviemakers and casting agents was to stop lifting weights – so his neck wouldn't look so thick and his body so pumped up– and stop wearing tank-tops and workout clothes everywhere, and get his hair cut.

David and Mickey hit it off and became a good team and trusting friends. When David's parents' dog died, Mickey got them another one – and they called it Mickey.

It would take a while but Unger's career strategy would eventually pay off and lead Mickey from obscurity to the awards circuit. To say thank you, Mickey gave David the Golden Globe award he won for *The Wrestler*.

But such glory seemed a long way away on *Spun*, in which Mickey played The Cook, a maker of the drug crystal meth who has set up a methamphetamine lab in a motel room and spends his days with spaced-out druggies. *Spun* was based on incidents from the life of the film's co-writer, Will De Los Santos, who once drove a meth cook around Eugene, Oregon, for three days.

The film is frantic, featuring a record 5,000 edits, bizarre, and suitably trippy, but Mickey swaggers through it at his own pace and steals the movie with a pair of memorable scenes. The first is comedic as The Cook delivers a monologue in an adult video store about the appreciation of "pussy," and the second is dramatic as he tells a story from childhood about his mother being unable to take care of him and wondering if she should have killed him.

The movie wasn't a financial success but it attracted plenty of publicity. Mickey did some promotion for it and the film got him back in the spotlight. Something else he got out of it was the striking pair of white cowboy boots he wears in the film. Mickey took such a shine to them that he had it written into his contract that he got to keep them at the end.

From Larry Charles, future director of *Borat* and *Brüno*, came the far less entertaining *Masked and Anonymous* (2003) starring Bob Dylan, in his first screen role in sixteen years, as Jack Fate, a legendary singer on a downward career spiral who makes a comeback at a benefit concert for victims of a war. Described as "arty-farty" by Mickey Rourke, the film, co-written by Bob Dylan, lacks structure and sense but features a great supporting cast who were clearly keen to work with Dylan, even if they couldn't all comprehend the script. Those names include Penelope Cruz, Christian Slater, Val Kilmer, Ed Harris, John Goodman, Jessica Lange, and Jeff Bridges, along with Mickey himself, well down the credits in the role of Edmund, a politician with a personal connection to Dylan's character.

There was a real-life connection, too. Dylan had been a longtime fan of Mickey's and describes in his memoirs, *Chronicles: Volume One*, being blown away by his performance in *Homeboy*. Meanwhile, Mickey already knew Dylan a little – the iconic singer had been a customer years earlier when Rourke owned Mickey and Joey's, his tiny Beverly Hills drinks, snacks, and paper stand – but the pair of them bonded on the set of the movie. Dylan asked Mickey for acting advice after finding himself unsure what to do with his hands in scenes where he had no dialogue, and Mickey told him to find some activity to do on screen. Ever since then, the legend has phoned Mickey every so often, usually late at night and always with the words, "Hi, it's Bob…," causing a confused and sleepy Mickey to grunt, "Bob who?" and getting the reply, "You know… Bob!"

From Bob to Robe: it was director Robert Rodriguez who hired Mickey next and their relationship was to be a key factor in

107

Mickey's return to the big time. Working for Rodriguez, first on *Once Upon a Time in Mexico* and then on *Sin City*, really paved the way for Mickey's later success. The Texas moviemaker had been a fan of the actor for years. In his late teens, he used to practice editing techniques by splicing together scenes from *Rumble Fish*, *Angel Heart,* and other Mickey Rourke movies that he loved. Even then, he dreamed of directing Mickey in a movie some day. But with little cash or connections, breaking into the film business would be tough.

But a lot can be achieved with determination and Robert went to great lengths to reach his goal, culminating in the future director selling his body for science experiments to raise the cash for his directorial debut, *El Mariachi*. The success of that movie led to him directing other hits like *Desperado, From Dusk 'Til Dawn,* and *Spy Kids* before he got the opportunity to make *Once Upon a Time in Mexico* (2003), a homage to the Sergio Leone westerns he had grown up on.

The film, set around an attempted coup in Mexico, featured Antonio Banderas as a gun slinging guitarist and Johnny Depp as a corrupt CIA agent. But there was also a role for Mickey Rourke – who had been suggested to Rodriguez by Depp – as a shady character named Billy Chambers. It was a small part but Rodriguez was so impressed with Mickey's work that he kept adding scenes so he could get more of Mickey on screen. He would write scenes for Mickey in his lunch break. An hour later, pages of great dialogue were waiting for the Rourke touch. Rodriguez even let the star act with his dog Loki in the film.

When they first met to discuss working together, Mickey

was holding Loki in his arms throughout their chat. Rodriguez thought that could work in the movie, too, and decided to add the dog (renamed Moco for the film, which was the name of the villain in Rodriguez's first picture, *El Mariachi*) to the script as Billy's only friend.

Something else Mickey brought with him to the shoot were his own clothes. Mickey has worn, or offered to wear, his own outfits in most of his movies over the years and *Once Upon a Time in Mexico*'s director – who was busy managing every aspect of the film – was delighted to get help with the costumes. He told Mickey to bring something "cowboy" and was impressed when Mickey showed up with immaculate two-tone suits and cool cowboy hats. In fact, the blue designer suit Mickey wears in his character's final scene when he is shot dead was so nice that Rodriguez didn't want to ruin it by putting a bullet hole in the jacket. So he spent more of the production's money creating a digital special effect of a bullet hole that was added in post-production in order to save Mickey's suit from being damaged.

Whereas Mickey's character gets killed – along with ninety-eight other characters in the film – his dog doesn't, and that probably made the movie more popular. For there is a well-known rule in moviemaking circles that you can kill any number of people on screen, but you will always lose the audience's affection if you kill a dog.

Mickey had a good time filming scenes with old pals Willem Dafoe and Danny Trejo but was especially impressed by director Robert Rodriguez's ability and enthusiasm. And the feeling was mutual. The director would spread the word to his moviemaking pals that Mickey had a thoroughly professional attitude now.

As he got to know him better during filming, the director realized Mickey was a troubled soul and had a lot of pain to draw on in his performances. Rodriguez filed that information away, thinking it could come in useful for a project he was in the early stages of thinking about, *Sin City*.

Mickey Rourke was gradually gaining a much better reputation for his behavior on film sets and he wasn't about to ruin that after being cast in a prestigious kidnap thriller starring Denzel Washington, *Man on Fire* (2004). He was professional in every way, such as sticking to the dialogue he was given rather than improvising different lines, as he had done frequently on other films. Mickey was also among friends here, working with co-star Christopher Walken and director Tony Scott. Mickey had long been one of Scott's favorite actors and the director, who likes to put actors in roles featuring elements of their own personalities, cast him as corrupt lawyer Jordan Kalfus, feeling Mickey could bring his own strange mixture of sweet and dark to the part.

Scott had planned originally to make the movie twenty years earlier and set it in Italy, which was the world kidnap capital at the time. That project fell through, but when the chance came again to make the film, he switched the action to Mexico because there was an average of one kidnap every hour in twenty-first-century Latin America, and 70 per cent of those taken turned up dead. Against that background, *Man on Fire* sees Denzel's former CIA operative hired as a bodyguard to a nine-year-old girl, played by Dakota Fanning. But he can't stop her being snatched by Mexican kidnappers, and the fight to bring her back leads to escalating action and intrigue.

Man on Fire took in $77 million at the US box office, became Mickey's biggest hit in the States, and would remain so until *Iron Man 2* earned that much in just its first two days on release. Another smash hit was to follow, and it really put Mickey's career back on track.

After making the third film in his successful teen heroes trilogy, *Spy Kids*, Robert Rodriguez was looking for something more challenging and he found it in a film version of Frank Miller's popular and stylish graphic novels about cool criminals, crooked cops, dastardly villains, and sexy dames, *Sin City* (2005).

For the key role of Marv, a hulking, hugely tall tough guy, he thought immediately of Mickey Rourke. The choice surprised Frank Miller, who was brought in as co-director. The comic book king said, "Do you mean that skinny guy from *Body Heat*?" But Rodriquez assured him the actor he had worked with on *Once Upon a Time in Mexico* was different now, looked physically imposing, could draw on his boxing years for the brute force needed in the fight scenes, and, most importantly, was a great actor with a tortured mind who could really tap into the frustration of Marv, who spends the movie avenging the death of his one true love.

Mickey would have to have prosthetics over his face to recreate the look of the character in the graphic novel but, as a fan of *Johnny Handsome*, Rodriguez knew his chosen actor had the ability to act through heavy make-up and bring emotion to the scenes. It was especially important that the acting not get lost amid the stunning visuals in the stylized film, which was all shot in front of a green screen with the backgrounds digitally added during post-production. With all the computers around the Austin, Texas, set, Mickey remarked that it was like acting in a NASA mission control room. But despite all the CGI trickery, Mickey's great performance gives the film a recognizably human element.

Mickey brought his own ideas to the role, giving Marv a tough guy walk apparently borrowed from an IRA gunman he had met many years earlier in Ireland. Because he doesn't like watching himself in movies, Mickey never normally looks at playbacks on monitors after filming his scenes. But he made an exception on *Sin City* because with all that make-up it was like watching someone else on camera. He broke another habit here, too. Mickey had rarely done action scenes up to this point – choosing to let his stunt double do them instead, rather than risk injuries – but he was happy to take them on in *Sin City*, particularly relishing a scene where Marv attacks a bunch of thugs with an ax.

Mickey was on fire in this film, getting many of his scenes perfect on the first take. The co-directors were impressed by how he immersed himself so thoroughly in the character. Miller, who has a cameo as a priest shot dead by Marv, would tell the crew, "He's going in," whenever he spied Mickey ready to inhabit fully the brokenhearted enforcer character.

Mickey responded well to working again with Robert Rodriguez. He thought the moviemaker was incredibly cool the way he would walk around the set in cowboy hat and boots, strumming a guitar and making up music for the movie's soundtrack and at the same time directing the action.

Playing the likable vigilante in *Sin City* brought Mickey some of the best reviews he had had in a very long time, and the huge success of the film – it took in $120 million worldwide – which also starred Bruce Willis, Jessica Alba, and Clive Owen, introduced him to a new generation of moviegoers. Mickey Rourke was hot again. He got an especially enthusiastic welcome in London from the crowds outside and the audience inside the UK premiere of *Sin City*, during which he sat next to Madonna and Guy Ritchie.

Mickey turned down a role in Guy Ritchie's 2005 crime film *Revolver* in order to work with director Tony Scott again in *Domino* (2005). The movie, full of dizzying fast cuts but not very involving, was based on the true story of the late Domino Harvey. The title character, played by Keira Knightley, was the daughter of film actor Laurence Harvey who left her glamorous and pampered life behind to become a gun-toting bounty hunter. Mickey plays Ed Moseby, the veteran bounty hunter who takes her under his wing and becomes a father figure. The character was based on real-life bounty hunter Ed Martinez, who served as a consultant on the film. Mickey's old friend Christopher Walken was also in the cast as a reality TV producer.

Scott had to fight to cast Mickey ahead of a flavor-of-the-month actor who was also up for the part. Mickey didn't think directors would still have to fight for him after the reports of his good behavior on *Once Upon a Time in Mexico*, but they did, and he was grateful to Tony Scott for doing so – and for having the script rewritten to beef up his part. That script, from *Donnie Darko*'s Richard Kelly, featured 123 F-words, a lot even for a Mickey Rourke movie.

Mickey hasn't always been complimentary about actresses, finding many of them needy, dumb, and self-absorbed, but he was impressed by *Domino* leading lady Keira Knightley, noting that the British actress was a real lady and very different from her Hollywood contemporaries, spending her spare time reading books, for example, rather than endlessly texting her friends. As he watched his poised twenty-one-year-old co-star be word perfect on every take, be friendly to everyone, give a convincing performance in a role which was something of a stretch for her, and always turn up punctually on set, he reflected just how different his undisciplined younger self had been on previous movies.

Just before *Domino* was due to be released, thirty-five-year-old Domino Harvey was found dead in the bathtub of her Hollywood home. The coroner later ruled that she had died from an accidental overdose of a powerful painkiller. Mickey, who had gotten to know her while making the movie and hit it off with the fascinating character, was hit hard by her death and attended her funeral, which he found profoundly moving. Domino never got to see the movie.

Mickey Rourke has not exactly been flooded with offers to appear in family-friendly movies, so he was pleasantly surprised to find himself filming *Stormbreaker* (2006), a spy adventure aimed at kids and teens. He was also glad to be back in London, one of his favorite cities, to shoot the movie, which was based on the first in a series of thrilling and bestselling books by Anthony Horowitz about a kind of junior James Bond named Alex Ryder. Newcomer Alex Pettyfer played the boy hero and was surrounded by a quality cast including Bill Nighy, Ewan McGregor, Alicia Silverstone, Andy Serkis, and Stephen Fry.

Mickey played the villain Darrius Sayle, a flamboyantly dressed tycoon with an elaborate plan to take revenge on the British prime minister for bullying him when they were at school together by killing all of Britain's schoolchildren, with a computer virus. *Stormbreaker* failed to make a killing at the box office, thereby foiling plans for this to be the first in a franchise of Alex Ryder films.

There had also been high hopes for *Killshot* (2005/2009) because it was based on a novel by Elmore Leonard, many of whose stories, including *Out of Sight, Get Shorty,* and *3.10 to Yuma,* had been turned into successful films. In a lead role originally intended for Robert De Niro when the movie was set to be made several years earlier, Mickey was cast as hit man Armand "The Blackbird" Degas, a menacing figure who kills anyone who sees his face. *Shakespeare in Love* director John Madden, whose perfectionist approach impressed Mickey, was behind the camera and hit maker Harvey Weinstein was producing. With all those impressive credentials, it's surprising that *Killshot* had a long and rocky journey to the screen. After filming in 2005, and undergoing reshoots and heavy editing, the movie sat on the shelf for four years, was finally released in only five Arizona theaters in January 2009, and came out nationally on DVD five months later.

Despite uneven pacing and some abrupt transitions, the film is rescued by a really good performance from Mickey as the half-Native American and cool contract killer who is rattled by the death of his younger brother during an assignment. He then makes the mistake of teaming up with Richie Nix, well played by John Gordon Levitt, a young, loudmouth crook who reminds him of his late brother. When their first job together goes wrong, two witnesses – an estranged couple played by Diane Lane and Thomas Jane – get away and flee into FBI witness protection. The Blackbird spends the rest of the film trying to track down and kill them, and the climactic shootout is breathlessly exciting.

It was rough on Mickey that after finally clawing his way to a lead role in a prestigious film, everything should fall apart through no fault of his, and hardly anyone got to see the movie in theaters.

Through all these setbacks, Mickey somehow kept the faith that one day a film would come along that would again enable him to show what a brilliant actor he is, and the world would sit up and notice. That day finally came when he landed the lead role in *The Wrestler* (2008). He plays washed up former wrestling star Randy "The Ram" Robinson who now fights in small-time bouts and supplements his income with part time supermarket work. When his health declines, he is forced to reassess his life.

There is a full chapter later in this book on the making of *The Wrestler*. Here I just want to point out that the success of that film prompted a string of offers for more great roles, which is what Mickey had wanted for years. But before he knew all those exciting opportunities would be coming his way, Mickey accepted a small role in *The Informers* (2009).

This one saw Mickey playing a thoroughly unpleasant character – a psychotic kidnapper who snatches kids for a gang of pedophiles. He has less than five minutes of screen time but is

creepily effective and oddly appealing as Rolex– and Ray-Bans–
wearing scumbag Peter, who involves a hotel doorman in his
latest kidnap scheme. Playing that reluctant accomplice role was
twenty-five-year-old Brad Renfro, the troubled former child star
of *The Client* who had battled drink and drug problems for years.
Mickey bonded with Brad on set, was impressed with his young
co-star's talent and keen to help him get his life back on track. He
invited Brad to come and stay with him in New York any time.
But Renfro never took him up on the offer. Shortly after filming,
the actor died of an accidental heroin overdose in January 2008,
one week before Heath Ledger died from an accidental overdose
of prescription medication. The movie was dedicated to Brad's
memory.

The Informers was also notable for being the first time Kim
Basinger and Mickey Rourke had starred in the same film since
9½ Weeks, but they didn't have any scenes together. When they
met on the red carpet at the premiere in Los Angeles, it was the
first time they had seen each other in twenty-three years. It was a
happy reunion because Kim had sent Mickey a letter saying how
much she had enjoyed *The Wrestler,* and he had been so touched
to receive it that reading the letter brought him to tears.

Basinger's character in the film is the long-suffering wife of
Billy Bob Thornton's Hollywood studio executive who has been
cheating on her with a TV newsreader played by Winona Ryder.
Rhys Ifans, Amber Heard, and Chris Isaak also appear in the sex-,
drugs- and violence-filled movie, based on a Bret Easton Ellis
novel, which follows a series of loosely connected characters
over a week in 1983. It seemed promising but didn't engage the

audience. The film was trashed by critics, its stars failed to promote it, and when the movie got shoved out into US theaters in the last weekend of April 2009 it bombed badly at the box office.

The Informers earned a dismal total of $315,000 from 484 cinemas that opening weekend and swiftly disappeared. Only four moviegoers showed up for the first public screening in Los Angeles. I was among them. But that dismal box office failure was to be followed by Mickey's biggest triumph...

Finally, after all the years of struggle, May 2010 saw the worldwide release of a film which would bring Rourke's talents to the widest ever audience. *Iron Man 2*, the splashy sequel to the 2008 superhero smash hit, saw Robert Downey Jr. return in the title role with Mickey as his new nemesis, a Russian criminal named Ivan Vanko who becomes the super villain, Whiplash. The hugely-hyped blockbuster sequel scored the fifth biggest opening weekend of all time, earning $133.6 million in its first three days on release in the US and Canada, putting it on target to earn even more than the first film.

Scarlett Johansson, Sam Rockwell and Don Cheadle were the other new additions to the comic book franchise, but it was Mickey's casting which got most of the media attention. Reviews were generally so-so, but most critics praised Rourke's memorable bad guy as one of the best things about the movie. Veteran *Los Angeles Times* critic Kenneth Turan wrote: "Mickey Rourke looks as if he's having the time of his life as Ivan Vanko, a.k.a. Whiplash, a disenchanted Russian with a grudge against our hero. Whether chewing on a toothpick, cozying up to his parrot or displaying more tattoos than the entire Russian mafia, Rourke's Vanko may look like a doorman at a bondage club when he gets into his Whiplash costume, but once he cracks those devastating whips the film takes advantage of his electricity."

Director Jon Favreau picked Rourke for the role because he knew the villain had to be a compelling figure capable of posing a threat to the hero, and there are few actors around more compelling or threatening than Mickey.

Not being a fan of the superhero genre, Rourke largely ignored the history of Whiplash in the Iron Man comic books and instead went with his own instincts about building the character, who Favreau had told him was of Russian descent and had been in prison over there. And so it was that a few weeks after casting Mickey, the director saw a news clip on the TMZ TV show of his actor getting a tour of a Russian prison as research for his *Iron Man 2* role. It came as a complete surprise because Mickey hadn't told him he was going over there to do that.

But thorough research is all part of his process and so the star went to Moscow's notorious Butyrka prison, known for its brutal conditions and hard-man inmates, fixed up a tour of the place from the guards, and, with real dedication to duty, he had himself locked in a cell and manacled in an ancient torture device. Later he met in his hotel room with a local ex-convict who had just been released after thirteen years. Mickey, who had been in a few jails himself, but not by choice, was fascinated by the tattoos with which longtime prisoners in Russia decorated their bodies to represent everything from their crimes to their sexual preferences.

On his return to the States, Mickey told Favreau he wanted

to appear in the film covered in (temporarily painted-on) prison tattoos, with gold teeth in his mouth, and having a pet cockatoo – all ideas that Favreau liked and okayed. Mickey had explained it was all about bringing humanity and dimensions to the part, so his character didn't end up a cartoon Russian villain, like Dolph Lundgren's Drago character in *Rocky IV*. He also wanted to speak only Russian in the movie – but the director swiftly rejected that request.

As well as learning a Russian dialect for the role, Mickey dedicated himself to losing the extra weight he had put on for *The Wrestler* and hit the treadmill while wearing a vest filled with weights, simulating the heavy armor he would wear in the movie. While Downey's character, Tony Stark, is completely encased in his metal suit, Whiplash has a half-suit of metal and leather showing off plenty of muscular skin along with those Russian prison tattoos. His hands and torso are wrapped in metal braces sporting neat weapons like electrified whips, as well as a glowing power pack chest device similar to the one Iron Man uses.

Favreau and Downey were impressed by Mickey's character choices and his dedication to the film. They happily shared stories of his prison trip with 6,500 deliriously approving fans when screening the first clips from the film at San Diego Comic Con in 2009. Favreau won big laughs from the audience, saying: "It turned out he was a sex god in Russia because the first film they got over there after Perestroika was *9½ Weeks*!" Robert joked: "Where else do you want to go if you're a sex god in Russia except a prison!" Asked about getting to work with Mickey, who, like him, had a second chance after self destructing his career, Robert said: "I barely know what to say. I thought I was eccentric. But he's something else."

He didn't mention quite how eccentric working with Mickey had been. To help his performance, Rourke had stoked up a bit of psychological warfare on the set in a bid to try and create some tension between him and Downey, similar to that which their characters felt. When former drug addict Downey was on the set, Rourke would sometimes blast the Amy Winehouse song "Rehab" from giant loudspeakers. Robert likes serenity on set but Mickey shattered that by repeatedly blasting out another loud song "Crazy" by Gnarls Barkley. The leading man is not a method actor but played along with those antics to help Mickey's process. When his co-star would try and act adversarial outside their trailers, saying things like "See you on the set, punk," Robert would reply, "Er, okay…bad guy."

But it all worked for the film which has become far and away the most successful of Mickey's career and made him a bankable star at last, enabling him to pick and choose his future projects instead of taking whatever offer is on the table. Quite a turnaround!

I've seen every movie Mickey has ever made. They've not all been good – in fact, many have been downright dreadful – but his star quality and undimmed talent shone through in every single one.

5
FEMMES FATALES

With a screech of car tires and a flair for the dramatic entrance, Mickey Rourke rolled up in his classic 1961 black Cadillac outside the hilltop church in Palos Verdes, California, where he was to say his wedding vows.

It was 31 January 1981, the sun was shining, and he looked quite a sight in a light purple suit, lavender shirt, and purple tie. Minutes later, he would walk down the aisle with beautiful actress Debra Feuer, whom he had met and fallen head-over-heels in love with almost a year ago to that day.

The proud groom had planned every aspect of the wedding himself, even designing Debra's ring of diamonds and rubies, his favorite jewel.

As his most precious jewel of all – the blushing bride – came into view, Mickey thought they would stay together forever.

How wrong he was.

* * *

Until Mickey was well into his twenties, he had never had a serious relationship. And then he fell in love at first sight with dazzling Debra Feuer. They met while working on *Hardcase*, a one-off TV crime drama in which he played a criminal and she was the undercover cop out to arrest him.

Between scenes, Mickey's eyes were mostly on Debra rather than his script. He would stare longingly at her and then quickly look away whenever she caught him gazing at her.

Feuer, barely twenty-one at the time, felt Mickey was shy and strange, but she was certainly attracted by his acting talent. She admired how he read his lines so truthfully, but without effort.

When the camera rolled, the awkward young man came to life and gave a combustible performance that reminded Debra of her acting idol, Marlon Brando. She invited him out to dinner at an Italian restaurant, purely as friends, one actor to another, but started falling for Mickey as soon as they began to talk. Neither of them touched their food. He described an idea for a boxing movie he wanted to make called *Homeboy,* and she listened spellbound. The attraction came as a surprise to her because he wasn't her type. She normally fancied Latin men.

Debra admitted later in several press interviews that she found it surprising that Mickey hadn't tried to kiss her on their first date. He was probably nervous because she had made a massive impression on him. Mickey knew that night that he wanted to marry Debra.

He proposed just a few months later, she said no, but he kept on popping the question and getting knock-backs. Debra didn't want to get married because she was focused on her career and, as they continued to date, she asked him to slow things down.

But she was young and in love and, when a love-sick Mickey gave her an ultimatum that she had to marry him or he would never see her again, she relented and accepted the proposal. By the time they were married, Mickey was on the verge of the big time: he had made *Body Heat*, was about to film *Diner*, and had started to get some high-paying movie offers.

The newlyweds bought a house in the Hollywood Hills and settled down to married life. Neither of them wanted children at that stage – Mickey's own turbulent childhood had completely put him off the idea of fatherhood – and they seemed perfectly happy with each other, at least at first. But it soon became clear they didn't have much in common. She liked to go out early and be in bed before it got too late. But Mickey was a night owl who didn't ever like to go out until midnight.

When *Diner* came out, became relatively successful, and brought him a head-turning first taste of fame, their relationship quickly soured. They had fights –mostly over all the time Mickey was spending out with his friends rather than staying home with his wife. When she called him up at the Beverly Hills office where he spent a great deal of time hanging out with his pals, Mickey would tell them, "It's my old lady," a nickname which infuriated and humiliated Debra. She would also complain about his extravagance: as soon as he got a lot of cash together, Mickey splashed out on expensive cars and his first Harley Davidson motorbike.

As the next few years went by and Mickey became more and more successful, Debra watched her husband change into a self-destructive star. There was always some drama going on in his career, such as his clashes with authority figures, which Debra attributed in later interviews to his rage at his stepfather. But there was drama at home, too.

Mickey was a jealous and controlling husband. He didn't want her to work, but wanted her at his side all the time. He would intimidate other actors if he believed they were paying her too much attention. Willem Dafoe was one who felt Mickey's wrath as he worked with Debra on the crime thriller *To Live and Die in LA*, in which she played the villain's girlfriend.

Mickey's eccentric behavior started to show itself. He was riddled with phobias. For example, he wouldn't go in the ocean because he was frightened a shark would get him.

Debra believes all that insecurity led him to the bad behavior which became a hallmark of his Hollywood career.

Mickey suddenly became very opinionated about show business and inflicted his views and his demands on his wife. He would see her working with actors and producers whom he didn't rate, and it really annoyed him. Mickey failed to share her idealistic, romantic view of Hollywood, seeing it instead as a giant pool of sharks.

Debra felt stardom eventually went to his head and that it left Mickey very cynical, sour, and disillusioned with the movie world. There were plenty of arguments and temper tantrums, which hurt the relationship.

Mickey had an old fashioned view of marriage, in which he wanted his wife to play second fiddle to her husband rather than having her own ambitions. But Debra wasn't that kind of person. She wasn't at all pleased. For example, during the period when he was preparing for and making *9½ Weeks*, Mickey got into character by isolating himself from her – going to live in a hotel suite and leaving her home alone, and becoming selfish rather than sensitive to her needs. The movie made him a superstar but his wife's mood wasn't helped by the fact that her own acting career was failing to catch fire.

The marriage really got into trouble when Mickey started to be seen out with other women, including model-actress Lauren Hutton who was in a car crash with the actor in his Mercedes as Debra waited for Mickey to come home. They had been traveling on the twisting Mulholland Drive in LA with Hutton at the wheel when she suddenly lost control and crashed into a mountainside. Neither of them was hurt but the car was written off. Mickey took Lauren with him to buy a new one the next day, and he was at the wheel this time when they drove away from the Mercedes dealership. Despite his womanizing image, Debra doesn't believe Mickey ever cheated on her. But he did seem to lose all interest in their marriage. He wasn't around and refused to try couples therapy.

Mickey seemed to prefer living in hotels to living at home, and Debra rarely visited him on film sets, choosing instead to practice yoga and meditation. They starred together in the movie *Homeboy* while they were estranged, but working together failed to bring Mickey and Debra back together as a couple. She filed for divorce in 1989 and the split was made final a year later.

Mickey felt bad about giving up on the marriage and how he had treated Debra, and although she only asked for her fair share in the split, he gave her everything. While she stayed in the marital home, he bought a new place fifteen miles away.

Debra Feuer's movie career never took off in the way that her husband's did, but her relationship with Mickey improved over the years and they are now close friends. Debra is currently a yoga teacher and has married again, to cameraman Scott Fuller. When she fell for Scott, Mickey insisted on meeting him so he could give her new man the seal of approval, which he did. He likes Scott and the couple's ten-year-old daughter Jessica Ruby. She calls him Uncle Mickey and he invites her round to play with his dogs. And when he finished filming *The Wrestler*, one of Mickey's first calls was to Debra, excitedly telling her he had just given the performance of his life.

After splitting from Debra, Mickey wasn't single for long. He fell hard for Terry Farrell, an up-and-coming actress who had been in a soap opera called *Paper Dolls* and who would go on to find fame as Jadzia Dax in the TV series *Star Trek: Deep Space Nine*.

Much like the marriage he had just left, this, too, was a stormy relationship with many bust-ups. But making up was the best part, and how they enjoyed that. They were a passionate couple who would disappear into the bedroom for hours on end. If Mickey looked tired a lot in this period, it was likely due to his marathon sex sessions with his girlfriend. Tactile Terry was always touching him, even when he was talking business with someone. People who saw them together remember her sitting at his feet or standing close to him, mouthing the words, "I love you."

But lest his legions of female fans would be upset to find he had a steady girlfriend, Mickey didn't advertise the fact they were dating. He would avoid being photographed with her in public and didn't mention Terry in interviews. The romance only went public when it ended. Eventually, the increasing number of arguments got too much for Terry and she ended their romance in a phone call. Mickey was in Italy at the time and just about to make a live appearance on a TV chat show. Minutes later, millions of Italian viewers watched, stunned, as the star guest broke down in tears on air saying how much he needed Terry and that he couldn't live without her. The couple did give it another try a short time afterwards but couldn't patch things up and split for good.

Mickey was romantically linked with several other women after that, including Princess Stephanie of Monaco, but that relationship never developed because Mickey didn't like the way the royal so often wanted to be the center of attention.

But he was soon to find a lesser-known beauty whom he would treat like a princess.

Carré Otis, a young model whose stunning face adorned covers of glossy fashion magazines like *Vogue, Elle, Harper's,* and *Cosmopolitan,* as well as ads for Guess and Calvin Klein, was cast as Mickey's lover in the erotic movie *Wild Orchid,* and the pair fell for each other on and off screen.

It was a part she so nearly missed out on because bigger names were offered it first. Brooke Shields was first choice for the role of young innocent Emily Reed but that failed to work out after Brooke made it clear that she was not prepared to do the nude scenes. Supermodel Cindy Crawford, who was looking to break into movies, was then offered the role, but eventually turned it down, deciding she didn't want such explicit sex scenes to be part of her first film. So in stepped Carré for her film debut. She may have lacked acting experience but her looks certainly weren't lacking.

Carré and Mickey fell for each other on day one, and it was an intense attraction from the start. With his divorce from Debra now finalized and the Terry heartbreak behind him, Mickey went all out to woo Carré, and she seemed equally wild about him. The stunner from San Francisco loved the actor's strength, intelligence, professionalism, and looks. Meanwhile, Mickey was utterly smitten, calling his co-star, "One of the most beautiful women God ever created."

When the pair shared an intense sex scene in the movie, there were many who believed they weren't faking it but actually made love for real on camera, a claim Carré later denied. Their romance didn't fizzle out after filming ended. Instead, their feelings for each other grew even stronger, and when Mickey proposed, Carré eagerly said, "Yes."

It seemed like a fairy tale – the movie star marrying the supermodel. The lovebirds were married on 26 June 1992 in beautiful Big Sur, California, and then had an idyllic honeymoon, taking off together on a romantic road trip, driving across America in his 1969 Road Runner convertible.

However, the honeymoon was soon over and the stormy years of marriage began. Both of them had equally explosive personalities – they were like thunder and lightning together – and frequent clashes resulted. Mickey wanted his wife to give up or scale down her modeling work, despite the fact that she had some big money contracts lined up, and that was something she was happy to do in order to spend more time with her husband.

Theirs was a passionate relationship in every way and they

were so devoted they each had tattoos of the other's name. But the tempestuous couple also generated plenty of ink in the tabloids. Their six-year marriage would be full of headline allegations of drug abuse and violence.

The first shocker came on 22 September 1991 when, while visiting Mickey in Sante Fe, New Mexico, where he was filming *White Sands*, Carré was shot by a gun registered to Mickey. She was rushed to hospital with a bullet wound in her shoulder and the police were called. Carré told the cops that her husband didn't shoot her and it had all been an accident: she had moved a black bag which, unknown to her, contained a loaded .357 Magnum and it accidentally went off. No charges were filed.

High drama like this was nothing new to Carré who came from a damaged background – she has said both of her parents had drinking problems, her first boyfriend was drug-addled, and she started using booze and drugs at an early age, while also battling anorexia and self-esteem problems. Carré left home at fifteen and moved to New York to model where her extreme dieting and drug use would gradually do her so much damage that she ended up needing heart surgery by the time she was thirty.

Carré has openly admitted being a longtime heroin addict, and Mickey spent a great deal of time attempting to get her off the drug. Those widely reported attempts ranged from booking her into a special clinic to beating up the drug pushers who were feeding his wife's habit. When laying into one of them, he apparently hit the guy so hard that his attack sent a stream of blood gushing high into the air.

But it was for allegedly hitting Carré that he found himself carted off by police on 18 July 1994. Mickey was arrested for "misdemeanor spousal battery," and was accused of kicking, slapping, and knocking down his wife during a chance encounter at the Los Angeles office of their publicist. He pleaded not guilty to the charge, which carried a maximum one-year jail sentence.

Mickey's mug shot was picked up by media outlets around the world. The actor was ordered to stand trial but the charge was eventually dismissed in December after Otis failed to show up for two court appearances when she was due to testify. "We had been attempting for several weeks to contact her through her attorney and were unable to locate her," said Mike Qualls, spokesman for the Los Angeles City Attorney's Office. She and Mickey had separated after the incident and he was banned from her fashion shows for a while. It looked all over for the couple. But on Valentine's Day 1995, they announced they were reunited and Carré moved back in with Mickey.

They tried to rediscover the magic and romance, and even made a second film together, the poorly received and little seen 1996 "thriller" *Exit in Red*. But the new beginning didn't work out and, after the dramas and disappointment all became too much, Carré left Mickey for good.

Mickey found it impossible to cope without the love of his life. He felt suicidal and was at one point held for observation for twenty-nine hours at an LA hospital. There was also the incident in the church when the parish priest talked him out of his plan to shoot Carré's violent drug pusher then turn the gun on himself.

Mickey tried to change his ways so Carré would come back to him, and started therapy as part of the plan to become a better person. In total, he waited nearly ten years for his beloved Carré to come back to him – but she never did. She moved on. They continued to speak from time to time but it just wasn't the same between them.

Carré happily conquered her drug problem and became a great deal healthier, not only with twelve-step-style recovery methods, running, and yoga, but also by becoming interested in Buddhism, going on retreats, doing voluntary work delivering medical supplies in Nepal, and generally having a spiritual awakening that helped her kick the drug habit. She put on a considerable amount of weight, but then re-invented herself as a plus-size model. Carré then tried to inspire others by sharing her recovery story on college campuses, lecturing about addiction, spousal abuse, and body image. Carré Otis is now away from the spotlight, happily living the quiet life in Mill Valley, California, with a new family. She has a second husband now, Matthew, an environmental scientist whom she married in December 2005, seven months after meeting him while out hiking. The couple have a daughter, Jade, born on 11 November 2006. The baby was a wonderful surprise as Carré hadn't had a period in six years and had been told she would never get pregnant.

As for Mickey, for a long time no woman came along to replace the gaping hole Carré left in his life. In the years after she left him, he never had dinner twice in a week with the same girl. With no steady girlfriend around, he would share his feelings with no one but his therapist and his priest and shared his bed most nights with his pet dogs.

But he hardly lived like a monk. Mickey had a string of one-night stands both at home and on his travels around the world. Over the years, he has taken a procession of women back to his room at Blakes Hotel, where he stays whenever he is in London, or to his homes in America. He claims to have had a sex marathon during one of his trips to the UK – boasting of bedding 14 women in one night.

Mickey was in fine flirty form while traveling the world promoting *The Wrestler*. Appearing on BBC TV's *The Graham Norton Show* in October 2008, he kept making cheeky advances, on air, to fellow guest Jessica Biel and asked if she was married – seemingly not realizing her boyfriend was one of the world's leading heartthrobs, Justin Timberlake.

At a December 2008 public Q&A in Santa Monica, California, during a festival of Mickey Rourke films, he responded to a question from a pretty girl in the audience by saying, "Look at you, you're not ugly. You know, there are things I like better than making movies…."

In late January 2009, Mickey hooked up with Chinese-American actress Bai Ling.

He was at Hollywood celebrity hotspot the Chateau Marmont Hotel with Sean Penn when he was approached by the skinny beauty. They had briefly met before when she attended *The Wrestler* LA premiere after-party a month earlier. Soon, they were all over each other and a brief romance blossomed in the following days. One thing they bonded over was their love of animals. Mickey loves his dogs, while Bai dotes on her cat Qiji.

But that relationship, like so many of his others, ran aground just a few days later.

The next famous face he was romantically linked with was Courtney Love, after they both won prizes at the *Elle* Style Awards in London in February 2009. But Mickey was quick to shoot down reports of a romance with Kurt Cobain's widow, saying, rather harshly, "I'd rather be on a deserted island with a gorilla!" At the same London event, Mickey had admired married British actress Thandi Newton and told her, "You're fit."

Days earlier at the British Academy Film Awards after-party, Mickey renewed his acquaintance with sexy blonde Abi Titmuss, whom he had met two years earlier at a music festival. The thirty-two-year-old – famous in her native UK for a taped sex and drugs scandal – was among the guests at the Grosvenor House Hotel bash and later claimed to the British press that Mickey had propositioned her at the event but she had refused to sleep with him.

Meanwhile, back in Hollywood, also distancing herself from Mickey was the young actress who plays his daughter in *The Wrestler*, Evan Rachel Wood. The twenty-one-year-old spoke out firmly to dispel growing rumors that she was dating Mickey, saying, "I'm not attracted to him. He's too old for me. Nothing ever happened and nothing ever will."

But rumors about Mickey's love life were constantly fueled by potential liaisons with a variety of high-profile women. On his return to the States, Mickey hung out with Paris Hilton at her twenty-eighth birthday party, but the night after that he was arm in arm and out on the town in New York with German model Manon von Gerkan, the former girlfriend of illusionist David Blaine. Then, when he went to Moscow in March 2009 to research his role as a Russian villain in *Iron Man 2*, Mickey was in the glamorous company of Russian boxer-turned-pop star Irson Kudikova. On his return to the States, he was passionately making out with twenty-four-year-old Victoria's Secret model, Eugenie Voldona, in the middle of a New York nightclub. More than a decade after his divorce from Carré Otis, he clearly hadn't lost his lust for models.

Mickey has always had an eye for the ladies and knows what he is looking for. Asked about his taste in women, he once said, "It's like what I look for in a horse ... I don't want a thick neck and short legs."

Randy Rourke boasted a year ago that was getting laid more often than he did in his late-1980s heyday. And that is despite, or perhaps because of, his favorite pick-up line, which apparently works surprisingly well. Having spotted a girl he likes the look of, Mickey has been known to say, "I can take you home and fuck you until you go crazy."

But just when it seemed he was settling happily for life as a swinging bachelor, Mickey fell for New York–based Russian model Anastassija Makarenko, twenty-four, who has become his steady girlfriend and turned him into a one-woman man.

The couple met on a photo shoot in the summer of 2009 and the swiftly smitten film star called her "a gift from heaven" and said he wouldn't trade her in for twenty Academy Awards. Rourke has met her parents, whom she's really close to, and they got along well. The parents gave the romance their blessing. Anastassija, whom he calls "Anna," shares Rourke's love of dogs and they got a Pomeranian together whom they named Tango.

She helped him with the Russian accent he used in *Iron Man 2*. Mickey worked for three months on it with a dialect coach and seemed to be making good progress, but when he tried it out at home on his girlfriend, she would laugh at his efforts. When the laughter turned to praise, he knew he'd finally got it right.

The reformed bad boy is determined to remain faithful to his new love and says he couldn't live with himself if he cheated on her. In May 2010 he told Britain's *OK! Magazine*: "I haven't fucked around on her. Sure, I could do something on the side but I've got to live with myself. That's something new for me – being honest in a relationship."

Despite rumors that they were engaged, proposing marriage hasn't crossed Mickey's mind. He added: "I haven't asked her. I haven't thought about it yet."

The movie star and the 5ft-11in model have been seen arm in arm everywhere together in recent months, from the red carpet at the *Iron Man 2* premiere to ringside at an Ultimate Fighting Championship match. It remains to be seen whether or not Mickey's latest leggy lovely turns out to be the ultimate love of his life.

What does seem certain is that Rourke's eye for a pretty face will follow him to his grave – and perhaps even beyond. For Mickey has said that when he gets to heaven, he hopes God says to him: "The girls are over there."

6
SIN CITIZEN

Mickey felt on top of the world late in the evening of 9 November 2008 as he strolled along Sunset Boulevard on his way into hip Hollywood nightclub Hyde while having his picture taken by an eager crowd of paparazzi photographers. The media had largely ignored Mickey for many years, but now he was relishing being back in the spotlight thanks to his comeback role in acclaimed new movie *The Wrestler*.

In interviews promoting the film over the previous few days, he had insisted that the bad-boy antics and temper explosions of the past were behind him and he was now a changed man. But it only took one question from the press pack that night to end the serenity and bring out his anger and sharp tongue once more. When asked about a recent article that claimed he was dating young actress Evan Rachel Wood, who played his daughter in *The Wrestler*, Mickey denied it and then made a nasty statement that suggested he still had some way to go to bring his demons under control. He snapped, "Tell that faggot who wrote that shit that I'd like to break his fucking legs."

It was a case of chivalry gone wrong but, like many times before, Mickey's big mouth got him in trouble.

* * *

Mickey may not have won an Oscar, at least not yet, but if there were a prize for craziest behavior by any living actor, he would have few rivals. Because despite his undoubted talent, Mickey has spent a lot of time acting more like an asshole than an actor. He has been the subject of more eccentric behavior stories than any Hollywood star since Marlon Brando.

Despite rumors to the contrary, booze and drugs have never been his big problem. It's his anger and his attitude that have most often let him down. The Incredible Hulk kept his temper better than Mickey Rourke, an emotional time bomb who spent many years rebelling against figures in authority and has never liked people telling him what to do ever since his domineering stepfather came into his life.

He would have been a much bigger name in Hollywood if only he had taken the advice of various representatives, directors, and producers who lined up some amazing star-making parts for him. Mickey turned down lead roles in some of the biggest films of the 1980s – *Beverly Hills Cop, Top Gun, Highlander, Rain Man, 48 Hours, The Untouchables,* and *Platoon* – and in the 1990s he rejected supporting roles in blockbusters such as *The Silence of the Lambs* and *Pulp Fiction.* He stubbornly chose to turn down hero roles and instead went his own way, building a career largely playing the only kind of parts that interested him: dark, edgy, and dangerous characters, outlaws, and various other bad boys.

It was a role he was playing all too frequently in real life as well, going around not with a chip on his shoulder but a boulder, and seemingly also carrying an edge of danger. Hollywood executives were scared of him because of the way he used to show up on set with an entourage of Hell's Angels, bodyguards, and various other tattooed tough guys. In fact, Mickey always seemed to have a pack of human Rottweilers with him. Growing up around gang members and boxers in Miami had instilled in him an admiration for such hard men and he felt a lot more comfortable in their company than around actors or studio "suits."

Many of these minders were on his payroll at up to $1,000 a week but, because Mickey wasn't being attacked by demonic stalkers or drug-crazed louts every minute, they mostly earned their money by fetching his cigarettes and projecting an unapproachable image.

Mickey was nothing but generous to the flunkies in his circle. In addition to the high wages, he even bought them motorbikes and cars. But he projected a menacing picture to the outside world.

When he walked into a restaurant, all macho attitude and tough guy swagger, people would flinch as if anticipating trouble. Neighbors in swanky Beverly Hills would be horrified by the noise and party atmosphere at his mansion, which would regularly have more than twenty motorbikes parked outside – Mickey's six Harley Davidsons, five belonging to his brother Joey, who lived in the guest house and flew a Jolly Roger pirate flag outside, and ten or so more belonging to visiting biker pals. Actor Richard Harris, who lived there before him, had warned Mickey that the neighbors wouldn't welcome him with open arms, but Mickey wasn't going to change his ways and saw it as their problem. Unsurprisingly, the neighbors on either side of him moved out.

Outraged Beverly Hills council members and residents

demanded the closure of Mickey and Joey's, the tiny street-side café he co-owned in the heart of the city's swanky shopping district, because he was using the posh street outside for noisy, night-time, high-speed Harley Davidson races with his leather-clad pals. It was also claimed that the presence of beer-swilling, unshaven, tattooed types in sleeveless T-shirts around the stand unsettled shoppers and frightened children visiting Le Grand Passage, the up-market arcade of shops where the café was located. Beverly Hills cops even impounded his Harley in the summer of 1989 on a "muffler violation," basically saying it was making too much noise.

Mickey's bad reputation grew as he reportedly developed social contacts with gangland figures and even showed up at a Brooklyn court to watch the 1992 murder and racketeering trial of Mafioso John Gotti, saying he was supporting his friend. Mickey had previously met Gotti while researching a project and said Gotti had been very generous with his time and insight. He and Gotti once had a bet on the outcome of a World Cup soccer match between outsiders Ireland, who Mickey tipped to win, and favorites Italy. They decided that whoever lost would buy the winner a watch. Ireland won the game and three weeks later Gotti's associates delivered to Mickey a beautiful and expensive wristwatch inscribed: "To Mick. All the best. JG." Suddenly, Mickey had gone from being the next James Dean to the new George Raft, a previous era's hot actor who had turned down star-making parts, took many tough guy roles, and associated with mobsters.

Mickey certainly had more time for Mob bosses than movie

bosses. In the 1980s, he mounted a brass plaque on the front door of his trailer which read, "All studio executives and producers to stay the fuck away."

Meanwhile, Mickey was just too flash for a lot of people's tastes, driving around in a gold-plated Rolls-Royce, the purchase of which was inspired by his Elvis obsession.

Timekeeping was another problem for Mickey and he missed early morning calls to film sets because he had been out partying all night. To stop that repeatedly happening on 9½ Weeks, director Adrian Lyne posted a minder outside his door to stop him going out late and to make sure he got to work on time.

At the height of his stardom, Mickey was so irresponsible that he couldn't even remember his agent's name. He would call up his agency of the time, CAA, and ask the receptionist, "Who's the little bald guy with the white Porsche?"

Mickey has offended plenty of Hollywood colleagues with outspoken comments, including Mel Gibson who publicly disagreed when Mickey claimed that acting wasn't a man's job. Mel said, "Mickey just thinks he is a tough guy in a black T-shirt." Mickey replied, "Mel's problem is that I am."

After the LA riots of 1992, Mickey told an interviewer that the films of director Spike Lee were partly responsible for the violent uprising. He was quoted as saying, "The blood of Los Angeles falls on those who instigated this revolt – the malicious prophets of black cinema and rap music, the movies such as those of Spike Lee and John Singleton."

Do the Right Thing director Spike Lee responded, "Mickey Rourke is a fucking asshole. He's a fucking redneck, motherfucking

143

cracker. I mean, he's an idiot. He's been riding a motorcycle without a helmet and he's punch drunk from being in the ring. How can Mickey Rourke say that me and John Singleton are responsible for the riots in LA? Like his films are responsible? He should get a fucking shave and take a shower." Actress Whoopi Goldberg also weighed in on the war of words, saying, "I think Mickey has taken a few too many lefts to the head."

In 2006, Mickey was reported to have raged against Tom Cruise, calling him a "cunt" following the A-lister's pronouncements against therapy. In TV interviews, the superstar had opposed psychiatry, as does his religion, the Church of Scientology, which has historically been at odds with the established medical and mental health community. Mickey had been in therapy for years, credits it with helping him make a comeback, and his one word response made it clear what he thought of Cruise's argument.

Barfly director Barbet Schroeder was so disgusted when Mickey suddenly dropped out, without explanation, of another film they had been developing that he put a note on the actor's front door saying he would never speak to him again – and he hasn't.

Outspoken Mickey has tended to say what he feels, regardless of the consequences. It meant he had no problem breaking the unwritten actor's rule that you never bad mouth your own films. For example, he called *Harley Davidson and the Marlboro Man*, "a complete piece of shit." And he's happy to say exactly what he thinks to people's faces, rather than behind their backs. He told the writer of *Harley Davidson and the Marlboro Man*, Don Michael Paul, in no uncertain terms just how bad he thought his script was and then told him to fuck off.

Rock stars are more known for smashing up hotel rooms than are movie actors, but Mickey appears to have done his bit to change that. Tycoon Donald Trump, owner of New York's posh Plaza Hotel, claimed the star caused $20,000 worth of damage to his suite during a 1994 stay and the room had to be closed to guests while extensive repairs were carried out.

The Tinseltown terror's behavior grew to be so laughably bad that Mickey eventually became a punch line for comedians and writers. Humorist Joe Queenan wrote a memorable article, which quickly inspired a spin-off TV special, in which he became Mickey Rourke for a day – dressing, speaking, and smoking in true Rourke style, and fucking with people like, well, you get the picture. He grunged up for the assignment by abstaining from bathing, shaving, or washing his hair for seven days beforehand. By the time his Rourke wildness was over, he had smoked eighty-two Marlboro cigarettes, threatened journalists with physical harm, sneered and snarled at passers-by, and blindfolded a female friend, *9½ Weeks*–style, before force-feeding her the contents of his fridge.

His history of explosive incidents has made Mickey a gift to journalists who have chronicled his career. But he hasn't always been so nice to them either. Mickey has undoubtedly become much better in his relations with the media recently – actually giving considered, honest, and emotional answers to questions – but it wasn't like that in the bad old days. There were many incidents around the world where he was dismissive of his promotional responsibilities. One typical example occurred twenty years before the triumphant visit to Italy promoting *The Wrestler* at the Venice Film Festival. Two decades earlier, he had left the same event with insults ringing in his ears. It all followed a moody press conference performance. First, he wouldn't speak into the microphone, then he got his translator to answer the questions for him because he couldn't be bothered to reply. Outraged by this insult, one of the Italian journalists stood up to complain, then walked out, urging all the other reporters in the room to do the same. He was applauded wildly but only six journalists followed him out of the room.

Mickey was also supposed to do telephone interviews during his forty-eight hours in Venice but wrecked that plan by taking the phone in his room off the hook. He departed Venice quickly by boat, leaving photographers fuming at the waterfront because he hadn't given them enough time posing for pictures. As Mickey sped away, several of the Italian snappers shouted after him, "*Stronzo!*" meaning, "You piece of crap!"

Mickey also disgusted reporters at the 1989 Deauville Film Festival by starting his press conference twenty minutes late, ending it forty minutes early, and saying very little in between.

But it wasn't just members of the press and the Hollywood establishment of whom he had fallen foul over the years. Mickey also got into trouble with the law.

The arrest that grabbed the most headlines was the alleged battery of wife Carré Otis, for which the charges were dropped after she chose not to testify. Mickey also spent a few hours behind bars in January 1994 following an argument that erupted after he helped bouncers throw some unruly customers out of

Mickey's, a Miami nightspot to which he had lent his name, status, and regular presence. He ended up in a shouting match with one of the ejected customers, with a large, riled-up crowd outside, and also with the police, who arrested him for resisting arrest – a charge later dropped. The irate film star later said in a press conference that someone had bad-mouthed him that night. He explained, "If somebody says 'Suck my dick' to me, yeah, I'm gonna get really mad and I'm gonna be offended by it. But I did not hit the individual and I did not touch him." The club's name was soon afterwards changed to XTC, apparently because Mickey's name didn't draw sufficient customers.

He was arrested again in Miami in 2007 on suspicion of driving a motor scooter while intoxicated, a charge later reduced to reckless driving and which, ultimately, went away.

Mickey, who had been clubbing at hot spot Mansion, was pulled over at 4:11 A.M. when his new green Vespa, carrying a sexy passenger on the back, allegedly made a U-turn on a red light and swerved in front of a police car. According to the police report, he started swearing when he was stopped.

Mickey's big mouth often got him into trouble, cost him work, and hurt his reputation. Speaking up and asking for his dog to get a part alongside him in the 2000 crime movie *Luck of the Draw* led to Mickey getting fired from the movie and made him a laughing stock in the film world. It all started during a discussion over his death scene. Mickey's character was supposed to walk into a warehouse, listen to dialogue between co-stars Eric Roberts, Ice-T, and Dennis Hopper, and then get shot. But he wanted an activity to do in the scene so he wouldn't just be standing around. So he suggested to the director, Luca Bercovici, that he should be carrying or stroking his pet Chihuahua, Beau Jack. They rehearsed it like that a couple of times, only for Bercovici to tell Mickey it shouldn't be done that way after all because the producer didn't want a dog in the scene. Mickey made his objections clear and they broke for lunch. Shortly afterwards, Mickey was let go, apparently for being difficult to work with, and was swiftly replaced by Michael Madsen.

It was a low point in Mickey's career, but there had been a much worse occasion many years earlier when his outspoken ways had made him, for a time, the most hated man in Britain. He just couldn't keep his mouth shut about his delight at being cast to play an IRA gunman in the movie *A Prayer for the Dying* and made some ill-advised statements that were interpreted as expressing sympathy for the Irish Republican Army's cause.

Just before the film's release in 1987, he issued a further statement including the following words, "As a concerned Irish-American Catholic, I wholeheartedly support the Troops Out movement and all efforts designed to assure equal human and civil rights for all citizens of Northern Ireland. There is no place in Ireland for British troops or second-class citizens."

The comments were especially insensitive because feelings were running extra high that same year following relentless IRA violence, including more murders of British troops and the Remembrance Sunday bomb which killed eleven of the civilians who had gathered at the cenotaph in Enniskillen, Northern Ireland, to pay their respects to the war dead.

With his grandparents coming from Cork, Mickey had long

been interested in the Irish Troubles and had very definite ideas about the economic and sectarian problems which would have motivated his movie character to pick up a gun and join the Provos. His research for the film included reading a biography of IRA hunger-striker Bobby Sands and going on a two-day fact-finding mission to Belfast – during which he stayed at the most exclusive hotel in the city.

Mickey claimed to have met IRA members who had helped him better understand the Northern Ireland situation and said after his visit, "I learned about the problem – how the Catholic minority's civil rights get stomped on like the blacks in America. How little boys see their grandfathers unable to get work because of their religion. I saw the graveyards filled with guys who died at 18, 20 or 22."

Meanwhile, he was said to be surprised to find there were a million Unionists in Northern Ireland because he had assumed everyone there was fighting to get the British out. *A Prayer for the Dying* had been due to open the 1987 London Film Festival but was withdrawn from the event due to ongoing real-life IRA atrocities. When it did open, the film flopped at the box office.

Clearly, Mickey had little grasp of the real situation in Northern Ireland but it didn't stop him speaking out anyway because he felt so passionately about the subject. Despite all the controversy caused that time, he foolishly returned to the theme two years later, and got into even more trouble. At the 1989 Cannes Film Festival press conference to promote his role as St. Francis of Assisi in the film *Francesco*, Mickey was asked if he was aware that Margaret Thatcher had quoted St. Francis when she was first elected British prime minister in 1979. He replied, "I really don't give a fuck what she has to say. Mrs. Thatcher should have given in to the hunger-strikers of Northern Ireland."

Then he let slip that he had given away a percentage of his fee for *Francesco* to "certain causes in Northern Ireland." Pressed by the British reporters to say exactly what those causes were, he made a vague mention of a fund for Joe Doherty, a notorious IRA gunman who had been convicted of murdering SAS captain Herbert Westmacott but escaped to the United States where he was currently fighting extradition back to Britain for completion of his life sentence.

The British press naturally had a field day with the naming of Mickey as one of Doherty's high-profile supporters and, the next morning, headlines such as "You Vile Brat" were screaming out from newsstands from Penzance to Perth. Incensed Conservative member of parliament Harry Greenway led calls for Mickey to be banned from visiting the UK ever again. Fellow Tory MP Ivor Stanbrook raged, "His statement in Cannes is proof that Mickey Rourke is helping to finance the IRA."

The British government had to answer the growing clamor for action against the movie star by stating it had no power to ban him under the Prevention of Terrorism Act unless the money had actually changed hands in Britain. Mickey was stunned by the outcry as he hadn't given any money to terrorists, but only clarified his remarks after he had been buried under a torrent of criticism. In a bid to calm the fury, he issued a statement saying, "My remarks were an emotional response, a little confused and certainly misunderstood. I have never given funds to the

IRA, Joe Doherty or anyone connected with the IRA and have no intention of doing so in the future. It is my desire to assist charitable organizations who provide help to the children who are innocent victims of the circumstances in Northern Ireland."

His manager and spokesperson of the time, Jane Katchmer, explained that Mickey had never spoken to Doherty but had received some correspondence from him about charities that help poor and homeless people, and had asked her to check out whether or not they were legitimate. When he arrived in Cannes, he thought she had done that and the money had been sent, while, in actual fact, she was still looking into it. She said Mickey had wanted to support groups that take children from the fighting areas to the United States on holiday and show them there are better alternatives in life than picking up a gun. Now, if he had just said that, he wouldn't have put his career and reputation at risk. But that's Mickey Rourke for you – he lives on the edge.

Mickey vowed never to spout off regarding politics again but couldn't help himself during George W. Bush's final year in the White House. Mickey was one of the few celebrities to speak up for the unpopular, outgoing president and said he felt he had done a great job. Just ahead of the November 2008 election, he said how much he admired controversial vice-presidential candidate Sarah Palin for her plain-speaking ways. Just days after the election he used the word "faggot" as an insulting term against that reporter who had written a critical story about him.

Even though he later apologized for his behavior, Mickey picked a lousy time to upset the gay community. The homophobia debate was raging around California that month as the State's electorate had just controversially voted against gay marriage. A few months earlier, TV actor Isaiah Washington had lost his job on *Grey's Anatomy* for using the same gay slur to characterize one of his co-stars, and his career has struggled to hit the heights ever since. Adding to the lack of sensitivity was the fact that Mickey was in an Oscar campaign against an actor playing a champion of gay rights – Sean Penn as Harvey Milk.

Things got worse for Mickey when reports emerged of him supposedly sending a leaked text message trashing Penn's performance in the film *Milk* and calling him "one of the most homophobic people I know." It seemed unlikely as the two are friends and Mickey had praised Penn's performance in a newspaper interview at the time. Mickey's publicist went into fire-fighting mode, insisting, "There is no Oscar feud between Mickey and Sean. They have known each other and been friends for a very long time. Mickey attended the New York premiere of *Milk* to support Sean and only has the greatest respect for him." She did not directly call the text a fake, but offered instead that "Mickey is completely unaware of the text."

Mickey called up Penn after the story broke to try and explain the situation, but Sean said he hadn't read it, didn't want to do so, and it didn't matter anyway. They remain on good terms.

Mickey needed to be on his best behavior in the run-up to the Oscars because it is well known in Hollywood that conservative Academy voters don't always fill in their ballots solely based on who gave the best performance but also consider how the front runners conduct themselves off screen. A profanity-laden speech at the British Academy Awards and other unfortunate public comments didn't help his cause and may well have cost Mickey some crucial votes.

But he was still making controversial statements after the Oscars, issuing a threat to E! channel host Joe McHale for making a joke on his show, *The Soup*, about Mickey's late dog, Loki. Mickey's considered response was, "That motherfucker is going to get a slap in the face."

Despite the occasional outburst, Mickey is doing better. For one thing, he no longer associates with the same rough-and-ready characters who used to make up his entourage. Neither does he travel with a bodyguard any more. He still has the odd inebriated night out now and again – like the time in June 2009 when he staggered out of West Hollywood club Guys and Dolls and had to lean against the nearest tree for a while before locating his taxi – but that's all part of the fun.

On a visit to London in 2010, he went drinking with a rugby team and decided to arm wrestle several of the players. He did well at first, but one of the hulking players was just too strong for him and tore muscle right off the bone in his right arm, resulting in a lot of pain and a trip to hospital.

The star still struggles to stay out of trouble but he's no wild thing these days. Certainly, the Mickey Rourke I have met is more pussycat than mad dog. And the actor himself would argue that the troublemaker reputation which has followed him for years is largely undeserved. After all, unlike various other badly behaved Hollywood stars, Mickey Rourke has never punched out a photographer, spat on a reporter, or beaten up another actor… and he's certainly never killed anyone.

Now a largely reformed character after many years in therapy, Mickey recognizes he was his own worst enemy for many years. Largely ashamed by those mistakes, the ex–wild man takes full responsibility for the hell he raised and the enemies he made. And in several interviews, Mickey has returned to the same basic theme: "I have nobody else to blame except Mickey Rourke."

7
DESPERATE HOURS

Mickey sat in the kitchen of his LA home drinking coffee and talking softly with his brother Joey's nurse, and facing the devastating fact that his brave sibling was about to lose his long fight against lung cancer.

The hospice nurse told him, "Joe shouldn't still be here. He should have left three or four days ago. The reason he's not ready to go is because he's worried about you. You have to tell him it's okay for him to go."

Joey had nearly died twice before from cancer, and had lived through three comas caused by motorbike accidents, but his famous brother knew this time really was the end. Mickey got up, shaking, and made the short walk to the bedroom where his little brother had been staying for the past two weeks. He put his arms around him, told Joey how much he loved him, and then said, "If you gotta go somewhere right now, you go ahead and I'll meet you there later on some time. It's okay, because I'll be okay, you understand?'

Joey then took his last breath – and died in Mickey's arms.

Since his brother's first diagnosis with cancer at seventeen, Mickey had done all he could to try and halt, then reverse, the inexorable march of the condition, including a mercy dash to Mexico for radical new stem cell treatment. He had always come to Joey's rescue when they were kids but he couldn't save him this time. Joey Rourke battled various forms of the disease over the years, but lung cancer eventually claimed him in October 2004. Mickey was shattered.

As Mickey admitted in an article with the *Sunday Times* in 2005, the one comfort to him was that in the final few weeks of life, Joey said how pleased he was that Mickey had changed for the better and was starting to get his life back on track. Joey had told him, with relief, "You've changed, bro', you're not so crazy," and the older brother cherished those words.

After the funeral, Mickey said a final goodbye to Joey as he threw his ashes into the sea – and noticed a flash of blue light on the horizon when he did so. Since then, whenever he sees a blue light, Mickey believes it is Joey waving to him. He still misses his brother terribly and, in the living room of his New York home, keeps a candlelit shrine to Joey where rosaries and photos of him surround a statute of the Virgin Mary.

The loss of Carré Otis from his life had been Mickey's first significant heartbreak, and the next was the passing away of his beloved, bearded biker brother. That tragedy caused him to question his faith in God for the first time. Mickey, who had briefly been an altar boy at the age of ten, stopped going to church for a while and no longer prayed with the same conviction. He couldn't understand why God would take his brother.

Two days after Joey's death, director Tony Scott, who had worked with Mickey on *Man on Fire*, called to offer sympathy. Scott's older brother, Frank, had died of cancer and so he knew the agony Mickey was going through. Tony proved a tower of strength at that difficult time and also provided Mickey with some work to go to, offering him a role in his new movie, *Domino*.

It was good for Mickey to be back from the B-movie wilderness, working on major movies again because for most of the past decade he had been in stuck in a career quagmire while suffering great personal misery during what he calls "my lost years."

But Joey had left Mickey with something – his spirit. Showing all the determination his late brother had possessed, Mickey resolved to battle his way back to the top.

* * *

Mickey quit boxing on health grounds, and thought he would be able to make a swift comeback to acting big time, but it didn't happen. Doors kept slamming in his mashed-up face. He still had the acting talent but, like his early screen idol Montgomery Clift, whose damaged face had to be rebuilt after a car accident, he was trying to relaunch an acting career with a very different look. Film history is full of stars springing back from obscurity, however, like Mickey Rooney, Marlon Brando, and Joan Crawford, to name a few. Mickey reckoned that in two or three years, he would be next.

Yet mainstream Hollywood didn't comply. Regardless of his ability or appearance, Mickey Rourke was damaged goods after his wild behavior in the past, and restoring the industry's trust and respect was not going to be easy. The film business had moved on, and Mickey ended up being cast in low-budget movies that were beneath him but to which his name and renown might add

some extra takings during their short cinema run or DVD life.
In a few short years, he had gone from starring with Robert De
Niro to acting alongside the likes of tattooed basketball bad boy
Dennis Rodman.

The major studios with their big pay checks weren't calling
anymore and he had to take very different screen roles: appearing
in a pop video for the Enrique Iglesias single *Hero*, doing a BMW
commercial, and providing one of the voiceovers for a video
game, the third installment of *Driver*.

As years went by and he still wasn't back in major movies,
Mickey began to think that all the people who had written him
off as a washed-up has-been maybe had a point. Being yesterday's
news was hell. It was humiliating for someone as talented and
proud as him to be getting little, or little seen, work as an actor. He
felt terrible whenever a passer-by would vaguely recognize him in
the street and stare, struggling to place the face and the name of
the former star. There is a scene in *The Wrestler* when Mickey's
character, Randy, becomes similarly upset at a delicatessen
counter, causing him to react in frustration by thrusting his hand
into a meat slicing machine. Art really was imitating life, because
Mickey is alleged to have reacted just as dramatically during his
wilderness years. He once described to an interviewer, but has not
discussed since, how, in a particularly dark mood, he deliberately
sliced the top of his little finger almost off, until it was just hanging
on by a tendon – and needed hours of microsurgery to have it
sewn back on.

To avoid being recognized all the time, he started doing his
shopping late at night in the twenty-four-hour West Hollywood

supermarket when there were few customers around to gawp at him. Extravagant purchases were a thing of the past as his money had run out. The big house and the big cars were gone, along with his good looks His entourage of hangers-on left him as soon as the money disappeared; some of them even took all they could carry out of the big house.

Court documents show that his LA home was repossessed after he couldn't make the monthly payments. And he owed various people money, not least the tax authorities. He was $60,000 in debt at one point and didn't have the money to pay the therapist who was by now treating him three times a week.

His businesses had gone bust, including Mickey and Joey's, the small Beverly Hills street-stand and candy store he had owned with his hairdresser pal Giuseppe Franco. Meanwhile, in an effort to stop all his wild spending, Mickey's accountants took his credit cards away from him.

With boxing gone and Hollywood not calling, Mickey was living in a $500-a-month one-room apartment, getting by with the money received from the rare acting jobs which came his way, as well as loans from friends, and the proceeds from selling his motorbike collection. Every few months, another of the dozen Harleys he had accumulated over the years would go at a greatly reduced price until there was only one left. When he couldn't afford the gas to put in his car, a 1963 Mini Cooper, he had to sell that, too.

He even wrote his way out of trouble at one point by composing poems and selling them. Mickey made an impressive $16,000 from selling eight framed, poster-sized poems displayed at a special Beverly Hills show. This is a sample stanza: "I should have been born a statue of stone, I'd have no pain, no place to call home." It's hardly Wordsworth but it was effective in helping the cash flow.

A poem which would have better summed up Mickey's life at this time when loved ones had left him, the studios no longer employed him, and photographers didn't want to take his picture any more was the best-known work by lyrical sixteenth-century poet Sir Thomas Wyatt: "They flee from me that sometime did me seek…." Mickey was now Tinseltown's forgotten man and, worse than that, most of the time, the pugilist-turned-poet was completely without the means to pay for everyday items. He had gone from eating in the finest restaurants to regularly dining at McDonald's.

Mickey was in a dark, dark hole. On the rare occasions he got some cash together and forced himself to go out to visit a busy and ritzy restaurant on a Saturday night, he found he could no longer get a reservation just by calling up and giving his name. Mickey was sick of going from millionaire movie star to hard-up has-been and wanted to be anonymous. Desperate, he called up an old friend who used to work on his cars and asked if he could fix him up with a job on a construction site. The pal laughed as if Mickey were joking and put the phone down.

Mickey would also phone Carré Otis, crying down the line and asking her to come back to him, but to no avail. He didn't have any big Hollywood dreams at this point. His only dream was that Joey would come back to life and walk in the door.

His respectability and hope gone, gloomy Mickey was widely

Sexy, clean cut and charismatic - Mickey in his mid-80's heyday.

A twinkle in his eye and stardom
in his future - Rourke in the early 80's.

Mickey Rourke with his ex-girlfriend, Terry Farrell.

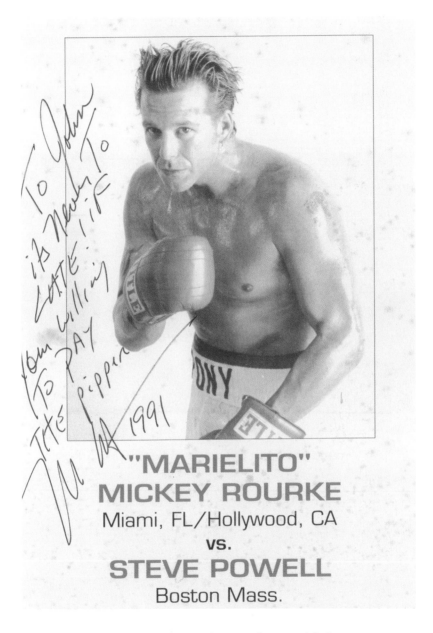

"MARIELITO"
MICKEY ROURKE
Miami, FL/Hollywood, CA
vs.
STEVE POWELL
Boston Mass.

The poster from Mickey's first professional fight in 1991,
autographed by Rourke.

The Boxer - Mickey is declared the winner after a 1992 first round knockout of Darrell Miller in Tokyo.

New love - Mickey shows off his stunning new girlfriend, Russian model Anastassija Makarenko at the 2010 British Academy Awards in London.

Mickey shows cowboy cool while
being interviewed outside the Vanity
Fair Oscar party in 2009

Photo by Stephen Gee

Rourke on the set of Once Upon a Time in Mexico with his beloved dog Loki, who appeared with him in the film.

reported often to fall to his knees and pray, asking God, "Please can you send me a little bit of daylight?" Things in his life would brighten up for a while and then quickly turn pitch black again.

After such a fall from grace, dark thoughts inevitably clouded his mind. He did consider suicide at this time but was stopped by a combination of his restored Catholic faith, the memory of how bravely Joey had fought for life, and a desire not to leave his dogs without someone to care for them.

With the closest relationships in his life, Carré and Joey, lost to him, Mickey felt alone. He had waited and hoped for Carré to come back to him for a long time, but something changed in him when Joey died, and he gave up waiting from that moment. He also stopped talking to his mother completely after Joey died, because his brother had been upset to the end about her turning her back on the sadness they both felt living with their stepfather. Thinking about his anger towards her, Mickey realized that, while he loved his mother, he didn't like her, and that he now gave his dogs more consideration.

When he felt upset as a child, he would go running to his beloved grandmother. That wasn't an option now that she was in her declining years, although she would live to the age of ninety-nine, only passing away in 2008. There was no way he was speaking to Gene Addis, he wasn't close to his stepbrothers, and his sister had her own life. But Mickey had his dogs, and they were a huge comfort. The unconditional love he received from them kept him going during such dark times. He has adopted a bunch of four-legged friends from shelters, mostly tiny Chihuahuas, choosing to rescue dogs that had been abused because their suffering reminded him of how he had struggled at the hands of his stepfather.

The dogs were great companions for Mickey, and became his new entourage. They filled an emotional gap in his life, too, turning his home into a much happier place. Mickey was unable to sleep in his bed for years after Carré left, feeling it was just too big and empty without her, and switched to sleeping on the couch instead. But as he took in more and more dogs, they crowded on to the sofa with him and eventually filled up his bed again, too.

Recent scientific studies have shown that the companionship of dogs brings about psychological and health benefits including lower amounts of stress-related hormones and the lifting of depressed feelings. His four-legged therapists really did the trick for Mickey.

His favorite of the bunch had been Beau Jack the Great, who became his constant companion. Mickey was distraught when Beau Jack died in 2002 and tried to bring him back to life, attempting to give the dog mouth-to-mouth resuscitation for forty-five minutes until friends pulled him away. When he knew the dog was gone, Mickey took Beau Jack's body to a church to be blessed. He fell into a deep depression afterwards and was only lifted from it by Beau Jack's daughter, a small brown Chihuahua-terrier mix called Loki, who took over as his best friend on the planet. She had been the runt of the litter and Mickey had fallen in love with her the second she was born. Often seen dressed in a natty sweater, Loki, named after the Nordic god of mischief, was his frequent travel partner and was always at his side in the *Sin City* to *The Wrestler*–comeback years.

Mickey was so reliant on the companionship of the dog he called "the love of my life" that he once spent £3,000 to have Loki flown to England to join him on the set of the movie *Stormbreaker*. He had to have her flown from New York to Paris, then Paris to London, and also to pay for someone to come with her, but it was worth it.

He flew with Loki from LA to Austin, Texas, to work on *Sin City*, keeping the dog in a case pushed under his first-class seat, but not far enough under for the liking of a flight attendant who kicked the case while saying, "Can't you put that somewhere else?" Well, Mickey wasn't having that and roared back, "Fuck you, you fucking bitch, there's a dog in there. Don't fucking kick it again." Startled, she did as she was told.

Loki racked up a few film credits herself, appearing on screen with Mickey in *Once Upon a Time in Mexico,* and she can be heard snoring in the background of his narration on *Sin City* as she was snoozing on his lap when he recorded the voiceover. Loki also can be seen in her master's movie *Masked and Anonymous*, walking around during Mickey's first scene.

Mickey once told his agent David Unger that if they were on a cruise ship and David and Loki both fell in, it would be the dog he would dive in and rescue, no question about it. The thought of losing Loki was unimaginable.

But in February 2009, just six days before the Oscars, at the grand old age of almost eighteen, Loki fell asleep and died in Mickey's arms. A couple of days later, a downcast Mickey went for lunch at New York restaurant Nello, where Loki had often enjoyed the Carpaccio, and fellow actor and dog lover

James Woods commiserated with him. The loss of Loki looks to be something Mickey will never get over and there are little reminders of her passing every day –morning at breakfast, for example, he no longer has to put down her side plate of bacon, which she used to love.

When another of Mickey's Chihuahuas, Loki's brother Chocolate, died in 2006, Mickey's casting-agent friend Bonnie Timmermann paid a special tribute by writing a children's book about the dog called *Chocolate at the Four Seasons*. It was based on the nine and a half weeks she spent looking after the dog for Mickey while she was staying at LA's Four Seasons Hotel and casting the movie *Blackhawk Down*. Chocolate would ride to meetings with her in a chauffeur-driven limousine and charmed the staff and guests at the hotel, including the chef, who prepared delicious meals for the Chihuahua. Chocolate liked his food and enjoyed a gigantic T-bone steak the night before he died.

Mickey has been left with deep emotional wounds by the death of his dogs. While filming scenes in *Iron Man 2*, he had someone hold up photographs of some of his deceased canines behind the camera so he could tap into the sadness the role required. Incidentally, he so liked the bird he shared scenes with in that movie that he went out and bought one just like it after filming, Sonny, who has joined his family of adored pets.

These days, Mickey's most frequent companion is Jaws, a scrappy white terrier-Chihuahua mix, so named because when Mickey first picked him up at an East LA pound and went to kiss the dog, it bit his lip, drawing blood and causing the star to need two stitches. "I'll take him!" said Mickey.

The other dogs living with him now are Ruby Baby, a white Samoyed who destroyed many pairs of Mickey's designer sunglasses and shoes in her first few months living with him; La Negra, a black pug who rarely sleeps but enjoys watching TV; Bella Loca, another Chihuahua-terrier mix with bad legs and other health problems who, when Mickey rescued her from a Texas shelter, had a nail in her head from some debris that flew around in a tornado; Taco Bell, a big-eared, brown Chihuahua; and Tango, the Pomeranian he got with his girlfriend Anastassija. Mickey hasn't always taken responsibility in his life, but he is responsible for his dogs now, and happy to do it.

They all eat well, enjoying meals like grilled pork chops, ground sirloin, boiled chicken breast, and spare ribs. The names of all his dogs, past and present, are engraved on a ring Mickey always wears. And when he dies, Mickey plans to have his ashes mixed with those of his dead dogs.

With the help of his dogs, his therapist, and his priest, Mickey was gradually able to pull himself out of the doldrums. Yes, he had lost his loved ones and his career was a train wreck, but Mickey wouldn't let this change of fortune beat him. He had never been knocked out in the boxing ring and he wasn't ready to be knocked out by life. Mickey has always been a fighter and now that he was against the ropes it was time to fight back. He wanted to earn back people's respect so that when he walked into a room, everyone would look over in admiration rather than pity.

The way to do it was to remind everyone what a great actor he was. All the hard experiences he had had in recent years could surely be drawn on to make him an even better, more interesting actor than he had been before. He decided that even if he was in a weak movie, he would give a wonderful performance and get noticed. Mickey had reached the acting summit in the first place by working his way up via small parts and, humbled by his time in the wilderness, he was prepared to do it again in a bid to climb back to stardom.

The former boxer would now learn to fight in a different way in order to secure his future. He resolved not to derail that ambition with self-destructive behavior, deciding he would stay out of trouble, not shoot his mouth off, and behave professionally at all times. With his spirits renewed and his face rebuilt – de-puffed courtesy of four lots of reconstructive surgery – Mickey set off on the long climb back to the top.

Helping him get there would be a younger generation of moviemakers – people like Robert Rodriguez and Darren Aronofsky – who had grown up as fans of Mickey and now found themselves in a position to hire him for their movies.

The decline of Mickey Rourke had been one of Hollywood's saddest tales, but the fallen star still had enough hope and determination left to give his story a happy ending.

8
THE WRESTLER

Mickey Rourke was laid up in a hospital bed at LA's Cedars-Sinai Medical Center recovering from an appendix operation, feeling pretty sorry for himself, and wondering where on earth his roller-coaster career would go next.

Suddenly, the phone rang in his room and the patient took the call that would change everything. On the other end of the line was Darren Aronofsky, an up-and-coming director about whom Mickey's representatives had often raved. He said he had a project he felt Mickey would be just right for and asked if they could meet to discuss it.

Mickey immediately invited him to come to his room at Cedars so they could talk, but Darren refused, saying he had a phobia of hospitals. Aronofsky suggested they meet instead at his office when the actor was better, but Mickey refused, saying he didn't like offices.

Well aware of Mickey's eccentric reputation, Darren wasn't at all surprised by that remark and they eventually agreed to meet when they were both in New York a couple of weeks later in a restaurant both of them knew. One of the most rewarding partnerships of each man's career was about to be launched.

* * *

The novelist F. Scott Fitzgerald famously once declared, "There are no second acts in American lives." But then, he never saw *The Wrestler*.

That film turned everything around for Mickey Rourke, transforming him from has-been to hot property. It's a story of great drama and emotion – but so, too, is the tale of how the movie was made.

Everything started with the writer, Robert D. Siegel. He had spent eight years as editor of one of America's most successful comedy publications, satirical newspaper *The Onion*, but eventually got the urge to try a different form of writing. He switched to screenplays but none of the comedy scripts he wrote seemed to work. So Robert instead set out to write something closer to the kind of gritty sports movies he enjoyed, like *Rocky* and *Raging Bull*.

The result was a film called *Paul Aufiero*, which follows the experiences of a car park attendant and self-described "world's biggest New York Giants fan" who gets beaten up by his favorite player on the team. The screenplay found its way to rising star director Darren Aronofsky, who had made his name with the stylish and edgy films *Pi* and *Requiem for a Dream*, and he seriously considered directing it as his next project.

But Aronofsky passed because his heart was set instead on making a movie set in the world of wrestling – an idea he'd had when he graduated from the American Film Institute and which was inspired by his observation that no one had ever made a serious movie about the sport. Aronofsky had been a fan of wrestling as a kid and one of his fondest childhood memories was of attending a match at New York's Madison Square Garden in the early 1980s.

He needed a writer for the wrestling film he was now ready to make and, as he loved the mood, dark humor, and sad drama of Siegel's writing, he invited him to meet him in a coffee shop where he pitched the idea to him.

The aspiring screenwriter was immediately hooked by the concept and ideas came pouring out of him when Darren got him a copy of the 1999 documentary movie *Beyond the Mat*, which follows several former wrestling stars still performing at local arenas but for little money and despite suffering with various health problems.

The pair agreed to collaborate and attended wrestling shows together where they talked to wrestlers, including veterans such as King Kong Bundy, Nikolai Volkoff, and Jimmy Superfly Snuka, along the way discovering a deep admiration for such guys and wanting to create a character that would exist as a tribute to them.

Robert, who makes a cameo appearance in *The Wrestler* as a fan getting an autograph from The Ram, worked on various drafts of the script over the next two years while Darren worked on directing *The Fountain*, a big-budget, hugely ambitious, time-travel romance that would flop badly at the box office, and the two would check in every so often and exchange ideas.

Casting was discussed at this stage and both men had only one man in mind for the lead role – Mickey Rourke. Both were big fans of his acting and Darren pointed out that Mickey's own personal mythology had parallels to the character they were creating, who by now was called Randy "The Ram" Robinson.

When Robert went back to work on the script, he printed out two pictures of Mickey that he taped to his laptop screen as inspiration – one from his handsome, younger days in *Diner,* and one looking older and beaten up by life at a recent movie premiere. By visualizing Mickey in the lead role, his script really started to flow and, after fifty drafts, it was more or less finished.

Siegel, who has since rewritten *Paul Aufiero* under the new title *Big Fan* and made his directorial debut with that film, which got a small theatrical release in late 2009, was ready to hand over his script for *The Wrestler*. He had been paid throughout the writing process by Hollywood studio Warner Bros., keen to develop the project and release it. But as soon as the studio learned that Mickey Rourke was the man in mind for the lead role, it lost interest in the movie. Their executives argued, and it was hard to disagree with them, that Mickey Rourke was no longer a box-office name who would guarantee a return on their investment.

But Aronofsky was willing to put his career and reputation on the line to fight for his first choice and felt he would be able to get the movie made somewhere with Mickey attached, even if the budget had to be lower than originally planned. First, though, he had to get Mickey interested in the movie.

Mickey was the first to get to the Greenwich Village restaurant at which they had agreed to meet and, not knowing what Aronofsky looked like, gazed out of the window and quickly worked out which of the arriving customers was the man he had come to see. Recalling his first impressions of the director,

Mickey commented during one of our discussions, "I saw a guy pull up outside on a bicycle in an orange crash helmet. I thought, 'What a fucking pussy.' He looked real Jewish and real smart and when he walked in he had a swagger about him like his balls were too big for his pants.

"He came over and smiled and still had a smile on his face while he told me I'd messed up my career. Actually he said, 'Listen, man, you're a really great actor who's just fucked up your career…no one wants to work with you,' but he told me he had a project I would be good for."

Darren outlined the story about a burned-out wrestler who was once a big star in the sport but is now a has-been living in a trailer park and reduced to dragging his battered body into the ring for small-time bouts, and seemed to capture Mickey's interest. Mickey had no respect for wrestlers and had long thought of the sport as a joke, but he needed a job and so kept quiet.

But then Darren shocked him by telling Mickey he was well aware of the problems Mickey had caused for directors on his earlier films and, if they worked together, he would have to be utterly compliant at all times and respect his authority.

"While pointing his finger at me, he said if I make the movie with you, you have to do everything I say, you never denigrate me in front of the crew. You can't go hanging out all night and I can't pay you."

The old Mickey Rourke would likely have told him to go fuck himself and his participation in the movie would have ended right there. But after years of therapy and better career guidance, he saw things differently now. No doubt Mickey was shocked by the comments but he admired the director's honesty. So many moviemakers had lied to him over the years and had later stabbed him in the back that he liked how Aronofsky was honest enough to lay his cards on the table up front.

Mickey took the script home – but hardly fell in love with it right away. He admits, "I read the script – and I didn't think it was that great." His first reaction to Randy "The Ram" was "that character is one pathetic son of a bitch." He also recognized that the character felt shame at his has-been status and Mickey didn't know if he wanted to get in touch with similar emotions within himself.

Mickey had trained at the Actors' Studio in the Stanislavski method, which encourages actors to personalize everything. So he knew taking the part would mean putting himself in a dark place emotionally by revisiting some painful moments from his own life. But he had faith that he was in good hands with Aronofsky and felt that together they could improve the script and make a very good film. "I'd heard a lot about Darren Aronofsky for a few years. People who work for me had said he wanted to work with me."

Mickey would come to consider the moviemaker to be among the very best in the business. "He reminded me of Coppola. He doesn't compromise. He takes chances. He doesn't make your usual Tom Cruise movie. He's resisted Hollywood's efforts to make him do lousy movies. That sounded interesting to me. I have respect for someone who they throw money at but he says no in order to do his own thing."

Mickey had some ideas for making the movie better and was

happy that Aronofsky welcomed his suggestions and let him rewrite sections of the script. He said, "One was the scene in the locker room when Ram and the other wrestler are talking about the pharmaceuticals. I had pumped iron with muscle heads at the gym for fifteen years and I saw a few things. It was very important not to hide what really goes on. These days the wrestlers are all chiseled up. There are physical requirements your body has to take on, a certain way to look, and people do many things that might harm them down the road."

As well as adding that scene where The Ram is shopping for steroids, Mickey punched up the dialogue where the wrestler pours his heart out to the daughter he abandoned. He also wrote the big scene at the end where The Ram says he never thought he would be back in the ring again, that he isn't as young or as good looking as he used to be. That scene was all Mickey, writing from his own life experiences. But despite all the similarities, Mickey has been keen to point out that he isn't playing himself in *The Wrestler*.

To prepare for the film, he had to come to understand the world of wrestling and learn all the right moves, holds, and throws so his fighting skills would look convincing on screen.

His boxing background was no help at all in preparing to play a wrestler. "The sports are as different as rugby and ping pong," Mickey explained. While boxing is all about hiding the punch, wrestling is about showing it with exaggerated swings, so he had to unlearn all his established ring technique, including slowing down to a more leisurely pace than he was used to in boxing. Wrestling is all about delaying the result and stretching out the story, whereas boxers just want to get it all over as quickly as possible.

"It took me a month and half to stop fighting like a boxer. They brought in some ex-wrestlers and they worked with me real patiently. I knew nothing about the sport – I didn't even know how to put my tights on."

But he soon learned wrestling required a discipline and dedication that he had never expected. Those were qualities Mickey needed as well, in order to pump up his body for the part. To acquire the physique of a wrestler, he had to gain 35 lb of muscle and achieved it by twice-daily workouts with an Israeli ex-cage fighter, including lots of weightlifting, and eating seven meals a day. He was also flinging himself around the ring learning to wrestle, mostly with coaching from the film's fight scenes choreographer Afa Anoa'i who had once been a member of a bad-guy tag team called the Wild Samoans and is the uncle of wrestler-turned-film star Dwayne "The Rock" Johnson. The actor quickly learned that while much that happens in the sport might be staged, the pain is only too real.

Mickey injured himself so severely in training for the film that he was carted off to the hospital on three occasions – but didn't tell the director for fear of losing the role. "I'm no spring chicken and I was getting hurt. I told my agent but didn't want to tell Darren. I had three MRIs in the first two months' training for this."

He blew out a disc in his back, badly injured his knee, and also severely twisted his neck.

"I don't like doctors. I was going to an acupuncturist for

treatment. After three weeks of hell, I finally went to a real doctor and he gave me anti-inflammatory drugs. I was fine after that."

But suddenly, during his training for the part, Mickey Rourke was replaced. It had not proved possible to attract financing for the film with Mickey in the lead role. Investors wanted a safer bet, an established movie star. So it was that Nicolas Cage came on board as the new star of *The Wrestler*. Within two weeks of his agreeing to do the movie, the funding fell into place with $15 million readily available.

Mickey's representatives were devastated, but Mickey took the news surprisingly well.

He explained, "I was really relieved. I knew Darren would want me to revisit some dark places for this role, plus I wasn't being paid, so when they said I wasn't in the movie any more, I was the only one who wasn't upset. Then something happened with the other actor and suddenly I was back on the film and it was back to the training for me."

He wasn't wildly enthusiastic to be back throwing himself around the ring and visiting those dark, traumatic places. When his agent called to tell him he was re-attached to *The Wrestler*, Mickey even replied, "Oh fuck, can't you get me something else?"

Apparently, Cage was available only for a limited period and didn't feel he had the time to bulk up his body into a wrestler's physique. He knew Mickey had been attached to the role earlier, and even called Mickey for his blessing before stepping into the part. In working on the script, he saw just how much the screenplay echoed aspects of the life of Mickey Rourke, with whom he had worked on *Rumble Fish* many years earlier but had lost touch with over the years.

After Mickey gave him the go-ahead, Cage started training but, the way he tells it, soon realized that the only way he could rapidly transform his physique into that of a wrestler was by taking steroids – something he wasn't willing to do. So he resigned from the film, called up Mickey to inform him of the decision, and said he hoped Mickey could somehow get the role back.

The fact that he did was all thanks to Mickey's enduring popularity in France, where even flop films like *Heaven's Gate*, *Year of the Dragon*, and *Rumble Fish* were hailed as cinematic classics. The only company that would step forward to support the movie with him in it was a French one, Wild Bunch. It proved a wise investment as they would make their money back many times over. *The Wrestler* earned $27 million in American cinemas and many millions more around the world and on DVD.

Wild Bunch provided the film's budget of almost $6 million and that gave the movie the green light, although, given the reduced budget, it would have to be shot faster and with fewer locations than planned. This would be bargain basement moviemaking, a thirty-seven-day shoot using thirty-seven locations and with none of the frills of major films. Mickey wouldn't have a luxury trailer or even a chair with his name on it.

But he would be a leading man again. On his first day of filming, the assistant director would shout, "Bring number one to the set…," and that was music to Mickey's ears. He hadn't been number one in a long time.

Mickey threw himself back into training and Darren would

frequently check on his progress, all the time pushing him to be the best that he could be. Aronofsky felt his leading man had been a little lazy in previous film roles, coasting through the parts without much effort. But he demanded total commitment from Mickey on this film – and got it, too.

Mickey recalls, "I wanted Darren to be proud of me. He kept yelling at me all the time. I thought, 'I'll show you, you prick.' So I learned all these wrestling moves and I soon grew to love the sport."

The star did six months of bodybuilding and three months of wrestling training to get in shape for the part. Many professional wrestlers and fans of the sport that saw the movie would later compliment him for having the look and the moves just right.

Due to the challenges of the reduced budget, the film's wrestling matches were shot at actual wrestling shows with a live crowd, in between the regular wrestling cards they were there to see. The crowds, who love the theatrics of the sport anyway, seemed psyched by the idea of a wrestling movie and they got into the required spirit.

As well as putting himself in harm's way by flinging his fifty-something body around the wrestling ring, Mickey Rourke literally bled for the part. At their first conversation about the movie, Darren had told Mickey about "gigging," a trick of the trade which sees wrestlers hide a bit of razor blade in the tape covering their wrists and sneakily pull it out at a key moment in the bout to cut themselves on the face so the blood will flow into their eyes and give the audience a dramatic spectacle. Aronofsky had told the star he would want him to gig in the film, and Mickey had been nervously waiting for that moment for months.

When it came time to shoot the scene, Darren told him he really didn't have to do it, but Mickey replied, "Fuck that, I'm cutting myself," and anyone who watches the film can see the results. Mickey did it as a mark of respect for Aronofsky, who had won his admiration for continuing to be honest with him all along. He explained, "When he said he wouldn't pay me, at least he said it to my face."

Mickey did eventually get paid for the film, but not that much above "scale" – the Screen Actors Guild union rate – and a long way short of his big-money paydays of the past. But this one wasn't about the money. "Darren and I gained each other's trust," added Mickey. "I like to work with directors that are smarter than me and are very well prepared."

But it wasn't all sweetness and light between director and star and the pair had several arguments during filming, about everything from the costumes Mickey would wear to the number of takes he would shoot. Aronofsky was always pushing for more takes, saying, "I want you to bring it," and when Mickey said that he just had, the perfectionist director replied, "Bring it more." He was like a boxing trainer asking his fighter for one more great round.

Once when he wanted to drain all possible emotion out of Mickey for a scene, he did something guaranteed to push the actor's buttons. Right before calling action, he implied that Mickey's beloved dog, Loki, who had been sick in recent days, had died. It wasn't the nicest thing to do, but it was certainly effective.

There was a certain amount of give and take between director and star but Aronofsky established his authority so that he got the final say each time. When Mickey declared he wanted to wear a hearing aid in the film, he had to fight like hell to get his way. Darren didn't want him using any method actor–style props. In fact, he considers not letting Mickey wear sunglasses his greatest achievement on the film! Mickey justified his choice by telling him about an old wrestler he had met who now wore a hearing aid and Aronofsky relented, but under-used it in the film, so we see the hearing aid only fleetingly.

These creative debates were all about making *The Wrestler* the best movie possible, and Mickey was coming to realize that his whole life had been leading up to playing this role. He certainly understood what the character, The Ram, was going through as a hard-up has been. He said, "Randy The Ram was somebody twenty years ago and so was Mickey Rourke. When you used to be somebody and you aren't any more, you live in what my therapist calls a state of shame. You don't want to go out of the house. I lost everything – my house, my wife, my credibility, my career. I even lost my entourage, which is when you know things are really bad."

Mickey Rourke was once shopping in a 7-Eleven when a man walked up to him and said, "Didn't you used to be a movie star?" It was a humiliating moment for the actor and one that is mirrored in *The Wrestler* when The Ram is mortified to be recognized by a wrestling fan when working behind the deli meats section of a New Jersey supermarket. That was the most difficult scene for Mickey in the movie because it brought out much of his own shame at how far he had fallen in his own life.

Mickey begged Aronofsky not to shoot the scene or at least give the character a different low-paid job, such as a dishwasher, where he would not have to mix with the public. But Darren knew it was a key moment in the movie and felt that Mickey could use his own pain to make it a mesmerizing one.

The moviemakers didn't have enough money in the budget to close down the supermarket and fill it with actors, so the store stayed open throughout the filming and real people would often come up to the meat counter and Mickey would serve them while the cameras kept running. As such, a lot of the deli sequences are improvised. Mickey actually got into trouble with the supermarket manager for writing the wrong prices down on the meat containers many of those customers were taking to the register.

Apart from genuine customers, most of the performers in the deli scene were Aronofsky's friends or relatives. The irritating woman who complains about the portion size is Darren's mother. But there were plenty of other interesting casting choices in the film. When Mickey was out with Aronofsky in a club one night, they spotted, standing by the bar, the he-man who would play the steroid-dealing wrestler in the film. Pointing at the hulking stranger, Darren said that that was the sort of guy he wanted in the part. So Mickey encouraged him to go over and offer the man the job.

Scott Siegel was the man in the right place at the right time and he certainly made the most of his opportunity. Mickey calls him "the one guy who ever stole a scene from me."

But it's no wonder he seemed so authentic in the part. For it later emerged that Scott Siegel had served four years in prison for trafficking steroids. A few months after the release of *The Wrestler*, he was arrested and charged with the same offence. According to court papers, officers found 1,450 bottles of steroids in his home, along with $70,000 in cash, and ledgers detailing his steroid dealing. Siegel attempted to flee after cops closed in on him, driving his Cadillac Escalade through a fence and smashing into five police cars while trying to escape the scene. His attorney, Barry Levin, would later describe it as a "road rage" incident. On 12 April 2010 the muscleman was given a sixty-three-month prison sentence by Judge Kenneth Karas – the judge who sent sprinter Marion Jones to jail in 2008 - after he pleaded guilty to possession with intent to distribute anabolic steroids and two counts of assaulting, impeding, and interfering with officers in the performance of their duties.

Some real wrestlers were used in the film, but they were mid-level draws like Dylan Summers as Necro Butcher and Ernest "The Cat" Miller, who played Ram's final opponent, The Ayatollah, rather than more recognizable superstars of the sport. The director felt that using Hulk Hogan or any of the other better-known wrestlers of the past would hurt the fiction of the story and pull people out of the movie.

Although Mickey didn't really get any staples in his body in the hard-to-watch fight scene with Necro Butcher, Summers certainly did. He was so pumped up for the movie that he fired the staple gun into his forehead five times just in rehearsals.

The Ayatollah was a fictional character but the fact that he was portrayed as evil, wore a skimpy leotard in Iran's national colors, and was played by an African-American actor rather than an Iranian one, as a nod to the sham-like nature of the sport, did not go down well with the Iranian government, which condemned the movie.

When representatives of the US film industry, including actress Annette Bening and Academy President Sid Ganis, visited Tehran in March 2009, they didn't exactly get a warm welcome. President Mahmoud Ahmadinejad's art and cinema adviser Javad Shamaqdari complained about various "insults and slanders" against Iran in recent Hollywood movies, including *The Wrestler*, in which Mickey Rourke's character smashes a pole carrying Iran's national flag across his knee.

But everyone outside Iran seemed to like the film and, along with great reviews for Mickey, there was plentiful praise as well for his two leading ladies. Evan Rachel Wood, one of Hollywood's fastest rising young talents, played The Ram's estranged daughter, Stephanie. Because her character and Mickey's were supposed to have been apart for so long, Aronofsky decided that they shouldn't rehearse together or even speak to each other before filming the first scene they shot together. The actors felt his artistic choice worked in the film's favor by making that first encounter between their characters twice as emotional.

By far the most emotional scene of the movie comes when The Ram is pouring his heart out to his daughter, telling her, "I'm just a broken down piece of meat." Using all the acting gifts that have served him so well since the Actors' Studio days, Mickey isolated himself for a while to prepare for the scene and when he felt he had reached the right emotional level, walked on the set and performed that scene to perfection. But the director wanted him to keep doing it again and again. He recalls: "I nailed it on the first two takes. Darren wanted to do more. But I'd shot my load, it was all over the room, I was spent, I'd got my shit in the can.

"We did more takes and Evan kept getting better in the scene, I kept getting worse. Then Darren said this word I hate – 'Dude…' he said, 'Dude, she's blowing you away and you suck.'

"I said, 'As far as I'm concerned, you got what you requested.' He said, 'You've got to keep giving it to me.' I kept trying to bring it for him and for Evan. It's rare you meet someone like Evan Rachel Wood. She's so focused and natural. She would go off, smoke twenty cigarettes, come back and do a great take. We were working together, you don't get that that often. I've got nothing but utmost respect for her."

That respect only increased after a scene where Evan ended up bleeding for her art, just as Mickey had done. In their big confrontation scene where Evan throws magazines and a lamp at her screen father, she also picked up a soft drink can to throw at him but cut her finger on it, and the blood poured out. Darren Aronofsky was concerned about the actress, and also worried about the limited shooting time they had left at the location. He said they could either call an ambulance right then or use superglue to patch up the wound and continue shooting. Evan looked over at Mickey Rourke, who was beaten up from the toll of filming the physically demanding movie, and said, "I guess we'll superglue my fingers!"

Her character's issues with her father struck close to home

for Wood, who didn't have much of a relationship with her real-life father. She would get together with him generally once a year and those were always frustrating occasions where finding common ground and communication was difficult. But Evan was so moved by the storyline of *The Wrestler* that it caused her to work hard at reconciling with her own dad. She hopes the film inspires others in similar situations to rebuild relationships with their own fathers.

Mickey didn't become a father figure to her – or a boyfriend, despite some wild rumors – but more of a cheeky friend. For her twenty-first birthday, which he helped her celebrate at the Toronto International Film Festival, he got her a cake with a pair of handcuffs in it. Evan remembers waking up the next morning handcuffed to a champagne bottle, but with no clear recollection of how that happened. But what is clear is that her performance played a big part in *The Wrestler*'s success and Mickey has continued to sing her praises.

Mickey's other female co-star, Marisa Tomei, also won respect from Mickey, from critics, and award voters, too, landing BAFTA and Oscar Best Supporting Actress nominations for her role as Cassidy, the stripper who captures The Ram's heart. Cassidy was written as a mirror image of Randy: she was also at the end of her shelf-life, getting older, and earning her livelihood on stage with a mask of a public persona.

Mickey had to get in shape and learn the right moves for his role as a wrestler. Similarly, playing a stripper also has its routines and requirements. So, as well as exercising and giving up bread prior to filming, Marisa worked out for weeks with a hula hoop so she could swivel her hips and shimmy perfectly for the part. But she turned down Darren Aronofsky's suggestion that she should perform in a real strip club in front of actual customers as preparation for the role.

Her revealing performance in the film was done in front of hired extras and the crew – but it was shot in a real strip club, Cheeques, in northern New Jersey. In fact, it was so real than Aronofsky – who, incidentally, had attended the same Brooklyn school as Marisa, Edward R. Murrow High – had to have the club cleaned before he and his actors could work in it.

Just as he pushed his other actors hard to do better and better takes each time, Aronofsky showed the same determination with Tomei, too. The pivotal dance sequence where she strips, gyrates, flaunts, and prances around the pole was actually the twenty-sixth take the director had demanded for that scene.

Many moviegoers watching *The Wrestler* wondered how the forty-four-year-old actress was able to make herself so uninhibited, loose, and free in stripping scenes that must have been nerve wracking to film. The secret could be found in her coffee mug. Marisa asked her personal assistant to keep bringing over her coffee mug between takes. But the actress doesn't drink coffee. She had tequila in there, and after a few swigs and a few swings around the pole, Tomei was able to let loose.

Along with the actors, another crucial element in the film's success would be the music. In summer 2008, a few months after finishing his work on *The Wrestler*, Mickey was driving around Miami when his mobile phone rang and the voice on the other end said, "Hey, it's Bruce."

Puzzled, Mickey replied, "Bruce? Bruce who?"

"Bruce Springsteen," said the rock star who had been a friend of Mickey's for more than two decades, after Sean Penn introduced them, but with whom Mickey had lost touch in what he calls his "lost years."

Earlier in 2008, Mickey had written Bruce a letter telling him about *The Wrestler*, saying how closely the storyline followed parts of his own life and adding how glad he was that he hadn't ended up like Randy in the movie. He wondered if Bruce would like to write a song for the film's soundtrack. Springsteen had already proved himself the master at cinematic heartbreak with his Oscar-winning song "Streets of Philadelphia" from the movie *Philadelphia*, and Mickey knew he could deliver another elegiac winner.

Bruce recalled, "Mickey told me a little bit about the character. He said some people invest themselves in their pain and they turn away from love and the things that strengthen and nurture their lives – and he told me this was a guy that hadn't figured that out. So I said, 'Well, I know a couple of those guys...' In the song, Springsteen sings: *Have you ever seen a one-legged dog making its way down the street? If you've ever seen a one-legged dog, then you've seen me...*

That night, The Boss was calling back to say, "Listen, I wrote a little something." The sad but beautiful song, which is called *The Wrestler* and plays over the film's end credits, is the perfect accompaniment to Mickey's heartbreaking performance. Bruce wrote it without having seen a frame of the film, but as Mickey explained, "He didn't see the movie, but he knows me." And as a favor to his old friend Mickey, Bruce gave the song to the makers of the low-budget movie for nothing.

After the track won a Golden Globe for Best Song from a Motion Picture, Mickey said, "'The Wrestler' will probably be my favorite song until I go to my grave. Bruce did me a favor and you can't put a price on shit like that."

It was a gesture repeated by another rock star pal, Axl Rose. The Ram comes out to the ring for his final fight with the Guns 'n' Roses song "Sweet Child o' Mine" blaring – just as Mickey did in his boxing days. Paying for rights to use the song in the film was way beyond the movie's meager budget, so Axl Rose gave permission to use his song for free to help Mickey, and is thanked for doing so in the end credits of *The Wrestler*.

With the movie finished and the music done, *The Wrestler* was ready to be unleashed on audiences, courtesy of a distribution deal with Fox Searchlight, the company which had scored big hits with other small films like *The Full Monty*, *Napoleon Dynamite*, *Little Miss Sunshine* and its latest acquisition, *Slumdog Millionaire*. When Fox Searchlight snapped up *The Wrestler* at the Toronto International Film Festival, critics and fans became curious to see what potential they had found in the film and in the comeback to leading-man status of prodigal son Mickey Rourke. But the reaction that mattered most to Mickey was that of the wrestling community.

His opinion towards the sport had totally changed thanks to playing The Ram, and he was desperate for the men who had really climbed into a wrestling ring to give the film their approval.

During my post-film Q&A with Mickey, Darren, and Marisa,

the director announced that one of those real-life ring legends, Rowdy Roddy Piper, was in the crowd seeing the film for the first time and, stuttering a little, the director nervously asked the big man at the back of the room, "W-well, w-what did you think of it?"

Roddy replied, "Yeah, I've got something to say," then he paused and the three guests looked at each other nervously during the moments of silence. But a moment later he paid the film glowing compliments, got emotional about how real it all seemed, and admitted he got "choked up" watching Mickey's perfect performance.

"When he started crying, I knew we were okay," smiled Mickey.

At the Los Angeles premiere of *The Wrestler* a month later, several more real wrestling stars of the 1980s showed up and, to Mickey's relief, they were the ones applauding loudest at the end of the well received screening. The star said, "Those wrestlers are a great group of guys with a special camaraderie. When they all said they enjoyed it, I couldn't have been paid a higher compliment."

The American critics raved, too, and Mickey was soon basking in the best reviews of his career with his work in the film called "heartbreaking," and "deeply affecting," and "among the great iconic screen performances." One review even said "skip the Oscar, give Rourke a Nobel prize!"

When the film opened in Britain a few weeks later, in early January, it was a similar story.

Sunday Express film critic Henry Fitzherbert declared, "The Oscar race for Best Actor ends here. Mickey Rourke is taking home the trophy for *The Wrestler* and, if he doesn't, I'll digest my DVD collection."

Awards buzz did indeed start to grow, and doors which had been closed to Mickey for years were suddenly opening for him again. *The Wrestler* opened on 19 December 2008 in just four cinemas in the United States but, powered by full houses and fine reviews, distribution had expanded to 700 by the time the Oscar nominations were announced in late January 2009.

Despite all the acclaim the film has brought him, Mickey Rourke still hasn't seen *The Wrestler*. He doesn't like to watch his films until a few years after making them because he gets irritated by things he wishes he could have changed or takes that were unjustly cut out and says otherwise he would be knocking on a director's door at midnight demanding answers.

But when he does get around to watching this one, he can allow himself to feel proud of a job well done. Mickey admits, "I gave all of myself in this role. It was the first time in a long time I gave all of myself. It was the first time I felt that since I was an acting student."

Once filming was completed, he had been keen to go to the wrap party and celebrate. But Mickey was so spent, so physically and emotionally exhausted, that he couldn't even get out of his chair. As he says now, "People used to ask me what's the best movie I ever made and I always said I haven't made it yet. But now I say *The Wrestler*. It's the hardest movie I ever made but it's also the best movie I ever made."

9
AND THE WINNER IS…

When Susan Sarandon opened the envelope and announced Mickey Rourke as the winner of the Best Actor award at the 2009 Golden Globes, it was the sweetest moment of Mickey's career.

Everyone sitting at *The Wrestler* table immediately erupted in joy. Darren Aronofsky and Marisa Tomei were beaming and, in her excitement, Evan Rachel Wood spilled her glass of champagne on Bruce Springsteen. Hearing his name called, Mickey's face broke out into a smile and he immediately embraced Springsteen. He hugged Leonardo DiCaprio on his way to the stage, tripped on the steps, then recovered his footing to collect the trophy from Sarandon, and turned to address the crowd.

Everyone in the room had risen to their feet in a rapturous, standing ovation – the only other winners that night to receive such a tribute were Steven Spielberg and the late Heath Ledger. He looked out at the sea of famous faces cheering his triumph, said, "Wow…," and, clutching the most prestigious award he had ever won, Mickey began a memorable speech with the words, "It's been a very long road back for me."

* * *

If things had turned out differently, walking down red carpets and winning awards would have been a regular occurrence for Mickey. But, as we know, things went south after his promising start. Or, as one director told Mickey's agent, "The guy was a great actor but he shot off all his own toes."

The Wrestler provided him with a comeback worthy of Lazarus and made Mickey a fixture at the glitzy and glamorous events that made up the Hollywood awards season of late 2008 and early 2009. With his stringy hair, dark glasses, flamboyant clothes, and little dogs, Mickey cut a fascinating figure amid the superstar glamour of these ceremonies.

The march towards awards began in early September 2008 at the Venice Film Festival where *The Wrestler* won the prestigious Golden Lion for Best Picture. That achievement marked the first time everyone involved in the film started to realize that audiences and critics were really responding to the film and to Mickey's central performance, which the festival's jury president, director Wim Wenders, called "truly heartbreaking."

The buzz continued to grow over the following weeks as more and more influential audiences saw pre-release screenings. It became clear that there was suddenly so much audience goodwill towards Mickey Rourke and, as the star showed up at Q&As and special screenings, and did the rounds of TV chat shows to discuss the film, it seemed he had a real chance of awards glory.

The only previous awards of any significance that he had won were 1983's National Society of Film Critics Best Supporting Actor award for *Diner* and the 2006 Best Supporting Actor prize from the Chicago Film Critics Association for *Sin City*. But now he was being talked about for the first time as a possible

Oscar contender – especially after he received a Golden Globe nomination in December 2008 for Best Actor for *The Wrestler*.

That month, the prestigious American Cinematheque paid tribute to Mickey's career by screening a series of his best films in Los Angeles. The season started with *The Pope of Greenwich Village,* and there was a delightful moment in the Aero Cinema lobby after that screening where longtime Mickey Rourke fans, delighted to see their hero celebrated at last, kept shouting out the memorable Eric Roberts line from that movie: "They took my thumb, Charlie!"

Mickey appeared in person at the final night of the tribute event, following a screening of *The Wrestler*, and seemed overwhelmed by the adulation from a sell-out crowd. He had received a similar warm ovation weeks earlier at a London Film Festival screening of *The Wrestler*. But there was a reason the world was warming to Mickey. Everywhere Mickey went during awards season, he charmed audiences and interviewers with real humility as he told his comeback story, owning up to his mistakes of the past, saying his career was damaged by his own self-destructive behavior, and expressing his gratitude at being back in the game. He would always make a point of thanking his therapist, his agent, and his priest for putting him back on the right path.

With praise poured on him from critics and moviegoers following the late 2008/early 2009 release of *The Wrestler* in cinemas worldwide, he was in good spirits in early January 2009 when arriving at the Beverly Hilton Hotel for the Golden Globe Awards, Hollywood's second most glamorous ceremony after the Oscars. He was one of 300 stars on the red carpet but, as the comeback story of the year, he garnered most of the media attention.

Mickey sat next to Bruce Springsteen at *The Wrestler* table where Darren Aronofsky, Evan Rachel Wood, and Marisa Tomei were also gathered, hoping it would be a great night for their film. They were not disappointed.

Springsteen took one of the first awards of the night when his title track from *The Wrestler* won the Globe as Best Song from a Motion Picture. In his acceptance speech, The Boss said, "First and foremost, I'd like to thank Mickey. Without him, I wouldn't have written the song. Thank you for thinking of me, thank you for your inspiration, and thank you, brother, for your beautiful performance."

Mickey was clearly touched and blew a kiss at Springsteen on the stage. He would say later that, at that point, it wouldn't have mattered if he hadn't gone on to win the Best Actor award because seeing his friend Bruce rewarded with a trophy was enough for him.

But the night was only to get better for Mickey a couple of hours later when Susan Sarandon read out the nominees for Best Actor in a drama – Leonardo DiCaprio, Frank Langella, Sean Penn, Brad Pitt, and Mickey Rourke – and then called Mickey's name as the winner.

He seemed nervous on stage at first but went on to give the sweetest and most memorable acceptance speech at the ceremony. The winner said, "I'm not a really good public speaker. I was kind of hoping Robert Downey would come up here and talk for me a little bit. But anyway... Several years ago I was almost out of this business and a young man got in touch with me and kind of put his whole career on the line by representing me – and he did one hell of a job. So I want to thank David Unger for having the balls. I want to thank his boss at ICM, Jeff Burke, for not putting him back in the mailroom.

"I worked with a really special director who had to really fight hard for me to be in this movie because he couldn't get no money on my name. Darren Aronofsky. I've said this before, like in sports, especially, which I can relate to, really great players or directors come around every thirty years and I really truly believe that Darren is one of those cats. He brought the best out of me. He's tough…and he's smarter than the rest of us, maybe not Steven [Spielberg], but, you know.

"We didn't have a distributor when we went to Venice, then Fox Searchlight came to our rescue, so I want to thank Peter Rice. Also, we had a wonderful cast, the beautiful and talented Evan Rachel Wood and Marisa Tomei.

"Axl Rose…we had no money, Axl stepped up to the plate and gave us 'Sweet Child o' Mine.' I'd like to thank someone who broke his balls a lot, the producer Scott Franklin. I'd like to thank Bruce Springsteen for everything…I love you."

There were a couple of mild profanities in his speech, which prompted US broadcaster NBC to activate the seven-second delay switch and fade the screen to black. But it was Mickey's closing remarks which would get the most attention and stick longest in the memory. He finished by saying, "I'd like to thank all my dogs, the ones who are here and the ones that aren't here anymore. Because sometimes when a man's alone, that's all you got is your dog – and they've meant the world to me. Thanks so much."

The dog tribute went down well with PETA (People for the Ethical Treatment of Animals), which in the days following the ceremony signed up the Best Actor winner as the face of its latest dog neutering campaign. Mickey was shown in posters posing with one of his Chihuahuas, Jaws, under his quote: "Have the cojones to fix your dog."

Working with the animal rights campaigners made him more aware than ever before of the vast number of puppies who get abandoned or put down because there aren't enough homes for them, and he eagerly spread the message of responsible animal ownership in subsequent interviews.

Mickey got a real thrill later in the month when he was presented with a career achievement award at the Santa Barbara Film Festival by legendary director Francis Ford Coppola. In a graceful acceptance speech, Mickey called *The Godfather* the greatest film ever made and marveled at the fact that he had been able to work with its director twice.

Soon there were plenty of other awards piling up on Mickey's mantelpiece. His work on *The Wrestler* won him a string of honors, including the Best Actor of the Year prizes from the Boston Society of Film Critics, Chicago Film Critics Association, Detroit Film Critics Society, Florida Film Critics Circle, Kansas City Film Critics Circle, Oklahoma Film Critics Circle, San Diego Film Critics Society, San Francisco Film Critics Circle, Toronto Film Critics Association, Utah Film Critics Association, and the Washington DC Area Film Critics Association.

He received nominations for the Screen Actors Guild Awards and the BAFTAs and now the much coveted Oscar nomination seemed a mere formality. Or was it? Winning the Golden Globe, voted for by eighty-five international journalists, was one thing, but would the thousands of Oscar voters really write down his name? The members of the Academy are a traditionally conservative, largely elderly group, and no fans of bad off-screen behavior. Were they really willing to forgive the sins of the past and reward his comeback performance? Mickey was unsure.

The Oscar nominations were due to be announced at 5.41A.M. on 22 January 2009. The night before, Mickey's manager, J.P. Parlavecchio, asked him if he wanted to wake him with good news. Mickey replied, "I don't know."

He woke up at 8.30AM, realized he hadn't been woken with good news, and said, "Oh fuck." He had recorded the nominations, immediately watched the playback to see who had been honored, and found that he was among the nominees after all. When he watched Forest Whitaker read out his name as the last of the five contenders for Best Actor, Mickey didn't let out a cry of delight but just considered himself "lucky."

It was his first nomination – and a sweet moment. In a statement, Mickey said, "I'm so grateful and appreciative of this incredible honor. I'm tickled pink." His rivals in the category were veteran character actor Richard Jenkins for immigration drama *The Visitor*, Frank Langella for his portrayal of disgraced president Richard Nixon in *Frost/Nixon*, old friend Sean Penn for playing America's first elected gay politician in *Milk*, and superstar Brad Pitt who aged backwards in *The Curious Case of Benjamin Button*, the year's most nominated movie with thirteen Oscar nods. *The Wrestler*'s only other nomination was Marisa Tomei for Best Supporting Actress. Hotly tipped Darren Aronofsky and Bruce Springsteen were both overlooked.

A few days later, at the Screen Actors Guild Awards, Mickey's momentum was halted when he was beaten to the Best Actor prize by Sean Penn, but he still won the majority of headlines the next day due to remarks made to reporters that night on the red carpet. The star of *The Wrestler* revealed he had been in talks about appearing at the WWE's (World Wrestling Entertainment) upcoming showpiece event WrestleMania XXV in Houston on 5 April, and hinted he could even fight six-time WWE champion Chris Jericho there. Showing pure wrestling theatrics, Mickey looked into one of the TV cameras, pointed a finger, and said, "Chris Jericho, you'd better get in shape…I'm coming after you!" He told another interviewer he was going to toss Jericho "around the ring like a tossed salad." Soon afterwards, Jericho would say that Mickey had made a big mistake and shown him a lack of respect, setting up the kind of war of words that is common in wrestling. Mickey is sure to have been offered more money to appear at the giant WrestleMania pay-per-view event than he got for starring in *The Wrestler*.

Meanwhile, having the star of *The Wrestler* endorse his organization seemed like a canny move on behalf of WWE boss Vince McMahon to counter some of the negative publicity wrestling had received as a result of Mickey's film – which shows bouts with pre-arranged outcomes, wrestlers using steroids and being crippled in later life. Mickey publicly praised McMahon for transforming wrestling from a sport for fat guys in Speedos to one for superfit athletes and said he wanted to do anything he could to support the wrestling community because its embracing of the movie had meant so much to him.

The prospect of Mickey grappling in the wrestling ring for real built into a huge media story and also saw him appear on CNN's *Larry King Live* show. Chris Jericho was also on the program and vowed to teach Mickey a few things in the ring that he never learned while playing a wrestler in the movie. Mickey took the high ground and avoided a war of words by praising Jericho, but left the door open for a possible showdown at WrestleMania.

Common sense took over a couple of days later when Mickey's publicist said he wouldn't be going into the wrestling ring for real. Paula Woods told the Associated Press, "Mickey Rourke will not be participating in WrestleMania. He is focusing entirely on his acting career."

Mickey said at a later Q&A event, "I have people I should listen to now. So I'm listening to them and trying to keep it all about the acting for now." Nevertheless, he couldn't resist, and when WrestleMania rolled around, Mickey Rourke was there in the crowd. He was expected to stay in his seat because as a condition of his participation in the upcoming *Iron Man 2*, that film's insurers had insisted he not get in the ring and start wrestling. So he got in the ring and started boxing instead.

As Chris Jericho was finishing a match, he saw Mickey in the crowd and began taunting the actor. Mickey got up from his seat, gave the jewelry he was wearing to the people next to him to hold, slowly walked to the ring, climbed in, took off the hat he was wearing and put it over a ring post, and then advanced towards Jericho in a boxing pose. The wrestler put up his dukes, too, but his fists weren't fast enough for Mickey who caught him with a punch. Then the former boxer threw a left hook which sent Jericho crashing to the canvas, much to the delight of the crowd and the international pay-per-view TV audience. Wrestling icon Ric Flair jumped into the ring, raised Mickey's arm in victory, and Mickey took the applause of the crowd before clearing off with a big smile on his face.

But back in February, it was a showdown in the awards ring he was focused on as he battled it out with Sean Penn for the two big remaining prizes of awards season, the British Academy Award and the Oscar. Following Penn's win at the SAG Awards, it was now a two-man race between him and Mickey. Penn praised his old friend's performance in *The Wrestler*, calling it "a beautiful piece of work" and saying that he wept while watching it. Penn had won the Oscar once before, for his role as a vengeful father in 2003's *Mystic River*, while Mickey was seeking his first win with his first nomination.

Mickey had put in a string of public appearances during awards season, while Penn kept a much lower profile. The two men met up for a drink at LA's Four Seasons Hotel a month before the Oscars and Penn wanted to look out for his old pal. He advised him to be very careful not to do anything that could be misinterpreted. The spotlight was on Mickey again and it was crucial he didn't give the media any negative headlines. Perhaps he should lay low for a while.

Some felt Mickey's recent visibility might hurt his chances, that he was starting to look desperate. Another turn-off might be that he seemed too much of a renegade to attract votes from older, more conservative, voters. There was also the claim that he was only playing himself in *The Wrestler* – before you can be declared the best actor, people have to believe you are actually acting.

By the time Mickey attended the annual Oscar nominees luncheon at the Beverly Hilton Hotel on 2 February, he was distancing himself from frontrunner status and claimed he didn't expect to win the Academy Award this year. "I'll probably be sitting out there clapping for Sean Penn," he told the press.

But after struggling to get a good table in decent restaurants not so long ago, he was grateful to be invited to Hollywood's most exclusive luncheon of the year. Eating humble pie, the changed star said at the event, "The biggest change since the nomination is the people I burned bridges with are forgiving me for the horrible way I carried myself for many years."

Rourke, along with all his fellow nominees, received a free Oscar sweatshirt, a book on the history of the Academy Awards, and a certificate acknowledging his nomination.

He flew to England a few days later where another big honor was about to come his way. On Sunday 8 February, Mickey Rourke was in London for the BAFTAs (British Academy Awards), looking resplendent in a shiny black suit and wearing sunglasses despite the heavy rain. As he joined fellow nominees Brad Pitt, Angelina Jolie, Penelope Cruz, and Kate Winslet on the rain-lashed red carpet outside the Royal Opera House, it was like watching luxury cars going through a car wash. Asked by the soaked reporters whether he minded the icy weather that greeted him, Mickey replied, "It's really cold, but I've been out in the cold for a long time."

But he was soon feeling the warmth and love of British voters as he won the Best Actor award, which he dedicated to one of his heroes and friends, the late, great actor Richard Harris. His cheeky and hilarious acceptance speech included a special thanks to Marisa Tomei, of whom he said, "She's a hell of a talent and it was very brave of her to take her clothes off all the time – I enjoyed looking at her."

The speech contained two f-words – the first of which came when he thanked Darren Aronofsky for "giving me a second chance after fucking up my career for 15 years" and the next when praising his publicist Paula Woods for having the hardest job in show business by "telling me where to go, what to do, when to do it, what to eat, what to wear, and what to fuck." Both f-words were bleeped out by the BBC. Host Jonathan Ross, himself just back on the channel after a suspension for inappropriate behavior, joked, "I'm afraid that after that speech, Mickey Rourke is now suspended for three months." Mickey further lived up to his wild reputation backstage by swigging champagne from a bottle while carrying his BAFTA in the other hand.

The press and the public lapped it up, but Oscar voters watching on their TV sets five thousand miles away may not have been so impressed by the return of the bad-boy image. A leading Hollywood executive who is no stranger to winning Oscars told Mickey that night that the expletive-strewn speech had just cost him the Academy Award by alienating all the conservative voters. In a backstage heart-to-heart, he told him he had done brilliantly by appearing so humble and modest throughout awards season but was now falling at the final hurdle by giving people a glimpse of the uncouth actor of the past.

There had been examples in the recent past of an Oscar frontrunner losing out on an Academy Award following bad behavior at the BAFTAs. In 2001, Russell Crowe berated the show's producer, Malcolm Gerrie, for cutting his acceptance speech for Best Actor. When it came to the Oscars just weeks later, Crowe's performance in *A Beautiful Mind* lost out to Denzel Washington's in *Training Day*. In 2003, Crowe's film *Master and Commander* was nominated for ten Oscars but there was no Best Actor nomination for its star. It all goes to show that Oscar voters are notoriously intolerant of bad boys.

But many Hollywood insiders were warming to Mickey more and more with each mention of how much he loved his dogs. As the awards and attention piled up for Mickey, so did the presents for his pooches. Friends and colleagues who knew the dogs were the way to his heart bombarded the actor with congratulatory gifts of dog food, treats, and accessories. I even sent him a mini black motorcycle jacket for Loki from Beverly Hills pet boutique Doggie Styles.

But an even more eye-catching outfit was quietly being assembled for the elderly Chihuahua. At the Oscars, Loki was due to wear a miniature white tuxedo and black shirt, a replica of the Jean Paul Gaultier outfit which Mickey was planning to wear at the ceremony. But Loki would never get to show it off on the red carpet. After a short illness, the seventeen-and-a-half-year-old Chihuahua, whom Mickey loved more than anything in the world died in the star's arms, just six days before the Oscars.

On the day before the Oscars, Mickey used his Best Actor acceptance speech at the Independent Spirit Awards to thank the thousands of strangers who had written him letters expressing their sympathy over Loki's death. He got choked up on stage just mentioning the dog's name. It was a bittersweet moment for still-grieving Mickey twenty-four hours later when he stepped onto the red carpet for the greatest show in showbiz without Loki beside him. But the dog was there in one way – his picture was displayed on a pendant Mickey wore around his neck. He told the assembled reporters outside Hollywood's Kodak Theatre, "She stayed as long as she could. She left me at a time when she knew I'd be all right. I'd rather have Loki another two years than an Oscar and I told her that."

Brad Pitt was the next of the Best Actor nominees to arrive and discounted his own chances while telling the press that when he was starting out in the business, Mickey Rourke and Sean Penn were his two idols in acting and so he was honored to be in the same category as them.

The three-and-a-half-hour ceremony, hosted by Hugh Jackman, got under way with Jackman joking about Mickey's use of colorful language at recent awards shows by telling Mickey he could say anything tonight because the TV broadcasters who normally have a seven-second delay had switched to a twenty-minute delay in case he won.

But it soon started to look as if it might not be *The Wrestler*'s night to win anything when, in the first Oscar presented, Mickey's fellow nominee Marisa Tomei was beaten in her Best Supporting

Actor category by Penelope Cruz. There was still a long time to go until the announcement of the Best Actor winner and Mickey couldn't sit still in his front row seat all that time. During a commercial break, he got up and sat on the end of the stage talking to Harvey Weinstein until an assistant director ushered him off and back to his place just moments before the ad break was over.

Eventually, once it became clear that *Slumdog Millionaire*, also a Fox Searchlight movie, was winning most of the other Oscars, it was time for the Best Actor to be announced. The movie world held its breath to see if the gold statue would go to Mickey or Sean and Michael Douglas ended the suspense by announcing Sean Penn as the winner.

Mickey led the applause and was soon blowing a kiss towards his friend when the *Milk* star had the good grace to end his acceptance speech with a tribute to Mickey. The Best Actor winner said, "I am very proud to live in a country which for all its toughness creates courageous artists who, despite a sensitivity that sometimes has brought enormous challenge, Mickey Rourke rises again – and he is my brother."

At his backstage press conference minutes later, Penn continued the tribute, adding, "What I think is sensational about Mickey is that he's simply one of the great poetic talents in acting. He quite literally had me weeping almost throughout *The Wrestler*. I've known Mickey for over twenty-five years. I can't speak for his consistent sense of me because he's an excellent bridge-burner at times. But we share a close relationship and he is someone I've alternatively looked up to and advised."

If he was devastated at losing out on the biggest prize after all that success in the build-up, Mickey certainly wasn't showing it publicly. He put on a white cowboy hat and happily hit the party circuit later that night, not showing any outward signs of being bothered.

He was happily chatting at the *Vanity Fair* Oscar party with Carla Romano, Hollywood correspondent for British morning TV show GMTV, who recalls him as a most memorable interviewee. Carla says, "Although he didn't win that night and had clearly knocked back a few drinks, he seemed seriously pleased to be there and to be part of the action. To be up there made him feel re-invented, re-born and his inner rock star came out in full force, added with a delicious humility.

"But with a touch of the rocker about him and being eccentric and champagne-fuelled does not really make for a safe live interview. As I was talking to Mickey, he became more than a little obsessed with my earrings – they were worth half a million dollars and he wanted them. As the studio crossed to me live they clearly saw Mickey trying to prise those gems off my ears – as a live broadcaster I loved that. He wasn't the usual post-Oscar interview. He was dangerous…you knew he was going to swear. But the earring theft came as a huge surprise. I laughed my ass off. I loved it.

"I loved him, too. He's true to himself and doesn't really listen to the publicist, which is rare in this business. I loved the outfit he wore, too. He looked like a cross between Noel Coward and Jon Bon Jovi. He rocked it. Seeing that outfit, you knew it was Mickey even before you saw his face.

"I had never interviewed Mickey before but he was once in my top five sexiest men. I was a big fan in the *9½ Weeks* days. I guess he was exactly what I expected – a little flirty, gentle mixed with rough and answering the questions with a dash of 'fuck' for good measure. He comes across as a bad boy but when you talk to him there is such a beautiful vulnerability in his eyes that makes you want to sit at a bar with him, hear all his stories and give him a huge cuddle.

"Comeback kids are always fascinating but when people rise so quickly and then fall as hard as Mickey did, people want to see the best for them. Mickey has had a hell of a time and plastic surgery made him seem like a freaky weirdo to boot. But now people see a good actor and someone who tried to claw his way back. He is so different to most actors. He is like a broken-down alcoholic genius who has got back on the wagon and is holding on for dear life.

"I would be very surprised if his post box is not jammed full of scripts now. When you are hot in this town you are hot. If he carries on being serious about his craft and getting his life together then Mickey Rourke will continue to rise. If he manages to stay humble, that is. But temptation to believe your own press is huge and can make you a dickhead. I hope he doesn't go that route."

Academy Award winner or not, dickhead or not, Mickey was back in the ring, a contender again, and a champ in many people's eyes. Mickey Rourke even beat President Obama to the Guy of the Year trophy at the June 2009 Guy's Choice Awards in LA. Announcing the two nominees, Jason Statham said, "One has lifted our spirits and given us hope...Barack has shown some promise, too. One has movie star looks, Mickey can act really well. The winner is Mickey Rourke – the leader of the guy world."

Mickey gave away his unusual trophy, a giant pair of antlers, to US servicemen in the audience, explaining, "What the fuck am I going to do with these antlers in my house? I would rather they be on the front of some tank in Afghanistan or Iraq where they're kicking ass."

It was the last event of a long awards season that had seen Mickey kicking ass and cleaning up – with just one major prize missing. So many fans and friends have told him he deserved the Oscar to add to his award collection but Mickey seems okay with the gap on his mantelpiece. As he told interviewer Barbara Walters in her special which aired on US TV immediately after the Oscars, the award would have been a great honor but it wasn't everything to him. He explained, "In the big picture, you can't eat it, you can't fuck it and it won't get me into heaven."

10
HITTING SELF-DESTRUCT

Mickey Rourke rocked back and forth on the floor of the closet in his Los Angeles home and thought about ending it all. Carré Otis had left him, his career lay in tatters, his money was mostly gone and he didn't want to be alive any more. He knew that suicide was a coward's way out and that as a Catholic he shouldn't even consider it but, in his desperation, Mickey just wanted to disappear. His retreat from the usual comforts of normal life was now so profound that Mickey had recently taken to sleeping in the closet, because he found hiding away in there more comfortable than being in his own bed.

All sorts of dark thoughts clouded his mind, and he reflected that he had never felt so alone and so unloved. Perhaps he would swallow a deadly amount of pills or put a gun in his mouth. Then he was joined in the closet by his favorite dog at the time, Beau Jack, who looked up at him sadly and whimpered. It seemed to Mickey that the Chihuahua was saying, "But who's going to take care of me if you go?'

That small noise from a little dog was enough to make Mickey banish all thoughts of ending his life and pick himself up from the floor. But he was going to need professional help – not just the loyalty of a loving dog – to pull him out of this pit of misery. Mickey had thought shrinks were just for crazy people. Now

Mickey decided to see a therapist, a man he simply calls "Steve." Fifteen years later, he is still seeing him.

Therapy helped Mickey understand that all the rage and frustration bubbling away inside of him came from the traumas he suffered in childhood. Those sessions with Steve also revealed that he had been living in a "state of shame," that he almost wanted to be invisible – feelings shared at times by his character in *The Wrestler*.

He also learned what he needs to do finally to get that emotional boulder off his shoulder and conquer the demons with which he has wrestled since those early days. With so many troubling issues in his head, therapy was clearly going to be beneficial, and Mickey is to be congratulated for seeking the kind of professional help that made him come to terms with his past and move towards a brighter future.

* * *

In the rest of this chapter, leading Los Angeles psychologist Yvonne Thomas gives her expert assessment, showing how a troubled childhood of the kind Mickey experienced can bring on issues of shame, self-sabotage, depression, and distrust, all of which can be carried throughout life.

Dr. Thomas has three psychology degrees, a private practice, and is a media expert who has contributed to books, major TV channels, and market-leading magazines, including *Cosmopolitan*. She has not treated Mickey but does work with many Hollywood actors, and suggests ways forward so that Mickey can continue towards making the kind of spectacular comeback personally that he has achieved professionally.

Dr. Thomas divides her analysis into five sections – childhood, relationships, bad behavior, depression, and the future. She starts by showing how the sadness of Mickey's early years has impacted his whole life since.

Childhood

Dr. Thomas observes, "The world may see Mickey Rourke as that out-of-control, tough, insensitive, devil-may-care, boxing brute of a man, but learning about him and his childhood shows the potentially real, inner Mickey Rourke. That is a Mickey who is still somewhat a little boy, in pain, scared and confused, one who is deeply longing for love, acceptance, enduring and consistent connections, as well as a visceral need for emotional safety and security.

"In working with patients for almost twenty-two years, I look at understanding how a person's past connects to the present. Sigmund Freud, known as the 'father of psychoanalysis,' stated that the most formative time of a person's developing self-esteem and identity was in the earliest years of life. The type of environment Mickey Rourke was raised in directly spawned parts of the man and can explain why he took the path he did.

"As a child, he would literally run away from the emotional pain and angst he experienced upon hearing and seeing his parents emotionally hurt each other and go seek refuge with his grandmother. His lack of a loving, emotionally-connected family helped build a foundation for him that unfortunately was based on the divisiveness and abuse he observed between his parents. Then, when six-year-old Mickey's family split up, he experienced even more loss, confusion and turmoil, especially when he was put in the middle of the tumultuous situation.

"As we know, his mother told Mickey that his dad would be joining the family in Florida after they were to move, while Mickey's dad refuted this and blamed Mickey's mother as the home-wrecker. His dad never did reunite with the family, which allowed Mickey to target his mum as the 'bad one' while idealizing and glorifying his dad.

"The complete extraction of Mickey's father from his youth probably felt like a gut-wrenching experience to him, replete with huge feelings of rejection and abandonment from his original primary male role model – especially because he was the parent Mickey had felt the closest to and idolized.

"It seems that Mickey innately wants and likes closeness – as evidenced by his long standing upset when people that mattered to him in his younger years were either not available physically or emotionally to bond and connect with. This was exemplified when his parents divorced and Mickey didn't see his dad for around twenty years. When his mom remarried, he experienced more loss, feeling left out, unimportant and forgotten by the one parent who still remained in his life

"Young Mickey received many negative messages from the most key people in his childhood about how they seemed to view him and his place in their respective lives. It would seem to Mickey that his mother saw him as a boy less lovable or likable for her to direct her time, attention or help towards in comparison to her new husband and his five sons upon whom she predominantly focused. Mickey's dad apparently reflected to Mickey that he was so unimportant and valueless to him that he completely eliminated the boy from his life.

"Mickey's stepfather possibly indicated to Mickey that he was so worthless that he could be his emotional and perhaps physical punching bag at times. Adding to all this upset, Mickey felt his mother didn't protect him from this abuse.

"Because of enduring at such formative ages so many experiences involving loss and physical and emotional abandonment, it seems quite clear to me that Mickey came to expect that loss and abandonment were normal for him. Likewise, when he was a bit older, Mickey would find himself zoning out from his new surroundings in Miami and was often a million miles away in his head, presumably as a way to deal with his burgeoning feelings of confusion, anger, resentment and disappointment.

"This seems to have been Mickey's way, though not a healthy one, of coping with his upset. Since his father was no longer in his life and his mother seemed unresponsive, Mickey apparently didn't feel he could depend on anyone for emotional support or comfort and tried to stuff his feelings inside.

"Mickey probably felt a great deal of helplessness throughout much of his younger life – and certainly during parts of his adult life. Even though he made attempts to express his feelings and ask for assistance, his needs and emotions repeatedly were ignored by others. In his attempt to fill his need for personal connection, Mickey was drawn towards and bonded with other lost and discontented peers, unknowingly creating a pseudo family for himself.

"Also, as a teenager and adult, he would dress in avant-garde, feminine garb, perhaps as a way to hold on to his softer side and perhaps as a way to fit in with the misfit peers he had formed connections with, while simultaneously toughening up his external self in reaction to preventing further pain or upset from the outside world.

"Mickey revered his father for his physical strength and physique, continually cherishing the one photograph he had of him – hence the shock Mickey felt when, at his own initiative, he came face-to-face with his dad two decades later and in that one-of-a-kind moment, experienced his father's fall from grace, from muscleman idol to weak older man.

"I believe there was one main pattern of repeated behavior Mickey adopted from his childhood experiences that explains much of why he has gone through such a lot of heartache and failure, often by his own hand. He has subconsciously replicated experiences involving loss and abandonment. Mickey is, no doubt, entrenched in this type of pattern as he experienced so much trauma related to loss and abandonment during his most formative, vulnerable years."

Relationships

Mickey Rourke's relationships seemed doomed to failure as he lacked the ability to trust anyone. That was due, Dr. Thomas argues, to the two most influential people in his childhood – his parents – abandoning him in different ways; Mickey's father by leaving the family and his mother by not being fully attentive to him while doting on her new husband and stepchildren. Mickey's love life has gone badly wrong with two broken marriages behind him and no steady relationships for many years. Is Mickey just not cut out for marriage or close relationships?

Dr. Yvonne Thomas offers her verdict, saying, "Patterns learned in a person's childhood can shape and direct the way the rest of one's life is lived out, for good or bad. Sadly, from his earliest memories, Mickey learned that loved ones can hurt each other with words and actions. He also ostensibly learned that families don't stay together and that sometimes a significant person may disappear from one's life entirely, like Mickey's father did for two decades.

"If a child grows up with a parent who is emotionally distant and is uncomfortable being close physically or verbally, the child may not get many hugs, kisses or loving words from that parent. Unfortunately, this youngster may grow up also feeling awkward with expressions of warmth or affection towards and from others, and may actually interpret the way the parent holds back from him or her to mean that the child is unlovable and unlikable – and not just with that parent, but with people in general.

"The unspoken message the child may take from growing up this way might be if Mom or Dad didn't love him, then no one else could and certainly not someone who isn't tied to the child by blood as a relative is.

"In Mickey Rourke's situation, the earliest messages he apparently received about his world were those of turmoil, unhappiness and lack of physical and emotional safety, given the overt volatility and tenuousness of his parents' relationship. It was a pattern he was to play out later in his own most significant romantic relationships.

"With his first major love, his wife Debra Feuer, he could not sustain the closeness very long, even though things were going well for him in his career and in his marriage.

"Instead, Mickey spent increasingly more time engaging in activities apart from his wife, many of which were destructive both to him and to his marriage, including hanging out with his male friends, drinking, possibly abusing drugs, spending a lot of money on luxurious purchases, and ultimately going out with other women.

"Furthermore, he displayed jealous, over-controlling behavior with Debra, phobias and insecurities that further alienated the couple and eventually culminated in their divorce.

"It seems that Mickey did almost everything humanly possible to sabotage the relationship he had, probably because being in something loving and free of turmoil and unpredictability was an unknown entity to Mickey and, ironically, probably felt even more scary and uncomfortable than the tumult he eventually injected into the relationship. Mickey had not really experienced being in any relationship that was happy and healthy very long. Thus, I doubt that he had any idea what he was doing or why he systematically was sabotaging his marriage.

"Again, Mickey sustained loss and abandonment when Debra left him and he seemed to have suffered tremendously with her departure. Similarly, in his next meaningful love relationship with another actress, Terry Farrell, things couldn't stay peaceful and stable for very long either. There was plenty of passion, apparently, but not just of the positive nature.

"Apparently, Mickey and Terry went through many break-ups and emotional highs and lows together, partly due to Mickey having to hide his relationship with Terry from his adoring female fans who thought he was single. It seems Mickey may have been tempted by pills and attention from other women in this period. So this two-year relationship was terminated as well, chalking up another mark in the 'loss' column for Mickey.

"After this, Mickey got involved with Carré Otis, in a very intense relationship. Carré would later become his second wife and was a woman with whom he would experience even more anguish and pain due to the disastrous combination of their respective demons and addictions. The ups and downs of their relationship were proportionally matched with amazing highs and horrible lows. Mickey and Carré allegedly went through physical violence and drug abuse and the relationship ultimately ended up with Mickey reportedly going into a psychiatric hospital after Carré left him.

"This loss may have been the hardest one for Mickey to comprehend or accept because he waited ten years for her to change her mind and reconcile with him, which never did happen. Alas, but true to form, Mickey sustained another episode of significant loss and abandonment to add to his pile.

"Presently, Mickey also remains estranged from the first most significant woman in his life, his mother, partly because she asked him to buy her a house when he became financially successful and largely because she didn't safeguard or emotionally care for him when, as a child, he reached out to her. In addition, Mickey's father died of alcoholism not long after Mickey, as an adult, had reunited with his dad for the first time in almost twenty years.

"In summary, it is no wonder, with the accumulation of all of these grueling and painful experiences of loss and abandonment, that Mickey would become so distrusting and reluctant to having close relationships with new people who could also potentially hurt him in one way or another."

Bad Behavior

Why has Mickey behaved so badly down the years, inflicting harm on his career in the process? Dr. Thomas says, "Mickey has a long history of torpedoing his life by engaging in behavior that has been damaging and destructive – often to those causes that have mattered to him the most.

"He created an irreparable chasm between his first wife, Debra Feuer, and himself by acting out in a multitude of egregious ways, was arrested for domestic battery against his second wife, Carré Otis, and while no charges were brought there he did engage in other misdeeds against her, and often defied authority and the law, sabotaging his own progress with his schooling, baseball, boxing, part-time jobs, off-Broadway shows and Hollywood bigwigs.

"Through his pro boxing contests, Mickey also sustained some irreversible damage to his box-office-appealing face.

"Largely because of his background, Mickey unwittingly has been undoing the good things in his life over and over again.

Various factors have caused and contributed to the star's self-destructive actions and roller-coaster experiences. It seems that he was mostly taught, directly and indirectly, to be distrusting that people or situations could remain constant and to not value or care much about himself. As a whole, Mickey seems to have learned to view himself with disdain and negativity and carry so much shame with him that unfortunately caused him to subconsciously continue to play out these feelings in new situations throughout his life.

"Certainly, Mickey did receive some positive messages about himself and loving interactions growing up, such as with his maternal grandmother and with some school chums but, overall, the influences were negative and that had an impact.

"Whatever defense mechanisms someone may use to shield themselves from reality, the monsters don't really ever go away. They are there, even if forgotten and out of sight, causing havoc in some form or another, directly or indirectly in one's life.

"I offer suggestions for sustainable, healthy changes later in this chapter. My hope from all of this is that insight can be gleaned and empowerment genuinely felt by Mickey and any others who sabotage their lives in whatever ways they do."

Depression

How did Mickey become such an isolated and sad figure? Dr. Thomas's response is clear. "It seems that the authentic Mickey Rourke has always been a sensitive person, one who actually feels more deeply than others may readily realize and one who craves to take care of others, especially those in need like his physically ill brother, troubled women or abused dogs. He also has demonstrated his loving, warm side that can connect with and care for those beings that pose no threat to him – such as those dogs and his brother, Joey.

"But as we have seen from Mickey Rourke's life story, a person of such intelligence, heart and talent can spiral down to rock bottom in his love relationships, career and life and even seriously entertain the idea more than once that suicide might be the best solution to his troubles.

"Mickey has experienced so many versions of loss and abandonment over the years – such as death, divorce, emotional and physical rejection and unavailability and failure. Those experiences became familiar to him and caused a lot of pain. As time went on and Mickey had been hurt enough times in his life by people that had greatly mattered to him, starting with his mother and father, he isolated himself from any further deep human closeness. When people got too scary, erratic or disappointing to depend on, he instead allowed dogs in to fill his enduring, core need for companionship, closeness and emotional security, but on a safer, unconditional love-type of basis, which dogs can often provide better than humans.

"Mickey had regressed back to a childlike state when he was in his closet and contemplating suicide but was convinced he shouldn't go through with it by his dog's cries to not be abandoned. It was like his own abandonment fears while growing up.

"Happily, Mickey abandoned the idea of doing away with himself and sought therapy.

"In spite of all the trauma he has suffered, it actually is a healthy sign that there is still a part of Mickey that yearns for closeness and comfort and which he has allowed himself to find through connecting with and caring for his dogs. I believe these relationships have been very healing for Mickey, providing him the safety, security and consistency he so rarely has experienced with people.

"It would be even better if Mickey could also experience how human relationships could provide some of these comforts and I will suggest how that might happen in the future."

The Future

So, will Mickey Rourke conquer his demons and find a happy and settled future – or is he going to screw everything up again? Dr. Yvonne Thomas remains positive. "There is hope for Mickey as his continues his therapy. Greater self-awareness and self-knowledge can hopefully help provide enough courage and commitment towards healing wounds and ultimately finding true inner peace, happiness and love.

"For durable, sustainable, healthy changes to occur in a person, it is critical to identify and understand the various factors that have led to their unhappiness and failures so that patterns can be targeted and broken, self-esteem saboteurs can be pinpointed and eradicated, and a person can feel deserving of and working towards self-love and love from others.

"Firstly, for anyone to attain real success in becoming an emotionally healthier person, one must be able to admit that you have issues that need to change. The good news is it appears that Mickey has accepted responsibility more than once about being the cause of many of his own problems.

"The next step is to actively be willing to do something about one's issues, whether that involves seeking therapy or finding another way to resolve one's dysfunctional thoughts, behavior and/or feelings. Again, Mickey has definitely taken this step, initially fighting his fears about going to therapy and in the fourteen years of sessions since then, apparently learning to face himself and his issues – which usually is the part of therapy of which a person is unknowingly most afraid.

"In furthering emotional growth it is imperative to look for ways to refute one's own negative, inaccurate thoughts, beliefs, feelings and actions that limit, diminish or harm oneself and one's life experiences. One powerful way to do this is by venturing out into the world in small steps and trying out low-risk ways to test the waters. This is what psychologists call 'reality testing.'

"For Mickey, his first step with reality testing might involve him connecting with other animal-lovers or dog owners, be it at a dog park or dog-training class, since there is already that built-in safe commonality of everyone owning and caring for their dogs. Experiencing non-threatening social interactions with people that can actually involve positive, bonding experiences and continuing to build from there with other experiences hopefully can provide Mickey the safety, security and evidence that some people can be loving, consistent and, maybe, even worthy eventually of letting into his life at a pace he can tolerate.

"Certainly for Mickey to heal effectively and move forward

in rebuilding a healthy self-esteem and self-image, he must be able fully and freely to grieve the losses and abandonments he has sustained in his life, whether self-created or through life's circumstances.

"Through the safety of his therapy and, hopefully, with some support systems including the comfort of his loving dogs and eventually some trusted humans, Mickey can release in productive, healthy ways the bulk of his pain, hurt, disappointment, anger and confusion connected to the upsetting events he has experienced.

"By doing this step, Mickey then can have more emotional space to heal the wounded little boy who still lives within him. From there, maybe for the first time ever, Mickey can learn how to see himself finally as someone who is truly worthy of love both from himself and from others, as well as how to be in a mutually supportive, nurturing relationship with others, at last being free from the shame, self-sabotage, depression and mistrust that has controlled Mickey's life for far too long.

"Despite experiencing a succession of losses and abandonment throughout his life, this is a man who has continued to show he still wants love and certainly has exhibited the ability to give love back.

"I commend you, Mickey, on having the courage and commitment to continue on your journey to find inner peace, happiness and love. You will find your goal is definitely worth it. As much as you have impressed people with your acting achievements and professional resurgence, your efforts to heal and love yourself are the greatest inspiration of all."

11
SOUL MATES

Macho Mickey, who so often plays fearless tough guys on screen, cried his eyes out on the day he got his left ear pierced. In fact, he was flinching with fear before the needle even touched him.

A witness to the comical moment was make-up artist and hair stylist Teddy Antolin, who befriended Mickey during the nine years he prepared him for various photo shoots.

Teddy recalls, "We were in the middle of a photo shoot in 1986 when Mickey suddenly wanted to get his ear pierced. This big lesbian, who looked like a man, showed up to do it and Mickey said he only wanted his left ear pierced because the right is gay, or something.

"Anyway, she didn't even get the needle close before Mickey started flinching. The piercing started, Mickey started to cry and his ear got all pink. I told him, 'Mickey, keep still, the needle's not that long, it's not going to go in your heart.' But he was like 'Aaaarrgh!'

"She finally did it but we couldn't resume the shoot until it stopped bleeding. After a while, I was like 'It's not bleeding.' But it wasn't until an hour or so after she left he was finally emotionally ready to be shot again."

* * *

Teddy Antolin, now one of LA's leading hair professionals, is one of many old friends with fond and amusing but occasionally disturbing memories of Mickey. He recalls Mickey having very definite ideas about his appearance. "Mickey was always very opinionated about that. He told me he had been to hairdressing school. He also got knowledge from his wife of the time, Debra, and from all over the place. He would sometimes bring his own scarves and shoes to use in the pictures.

"Mickey certainly knew how to work that hair of his. He would always comb his own hair and then I'd fine-tune it. He wanted it to look like it wasn't combed, like he'd done it with his fingers, even though it had taken fifteen minutes to get to that point.

"The only advice I gave him with make-up was 'Keep it light' – but he never wanted to. He always liked to wear a lot of make-up in photos. He took contouring to an extreme level and really liked doing eyebrows, jaw lines, cheekbones, and giving himself a little color in his cheeks.

"I know he didn't watch his own films but he always looked at the Polaroids taken during his photo shoots, to see how things were progressing.

"Mickey was really sexy back then, with a great smile. He is a star because he has that 'X' factor, that deliciousness. But he was insecure. I don't think he really liked the way he looked. Mickey had a little bit of acne, he had some acne scars. I detected a lot of insecurity in him. He never projected it but it was just there. I can just tell. Nobody else picked up on it but me.

"I think he wanted to look more Italian – anything but Irish! He wanted to look smoldering. I think that's why he loved the make-up so much and then he went into the plastic surgery. I know why he did that – he wanted cheekbones, he wanted a jaw line.

The first thing he did was the cheek implants. I was on the road with David Bowie in 1990 and his record company threw a big party for David in a Los Angeles restaurant called 72 Market Street. Terry Farrell, Mickey's ex-girlfriend, came with me to the party and it was lots of fun.

"I went up to Mickey there and I pinched his cheek, which I always did to say hello. I didn't know he'd had them done until I walked away and Terry said, 'You pinched his implant – he's just had implants!' That was the beginning of it; from then on I would see him around Hollywood and the look got worse and worse."

It's interesting at this point to note that Mickey's ex-wife Debra Feuer publicly claimed that Mickey got cheek implants around this period but said when she challenged him about it at the time he told her his face was swollen because he'd had his molar teeth removed. He said the same when there was press speculation about why his face looked different in the film *Wild Orchid*.

Teddy Antolin also remembers Mickey's behavior around this time. He says, "Also, Mickey wasn't being so likable towards the end of the period I worked with him, which was around 1982 to 1991. I think he turned into a bad boy. That happens in Hollywood. After doing the movies he did he was like a rebel. He wasn't like Patrick Swayze and those clean-cut guys of the 1980s. I think he started to take on the rebel personality of the characters he played in the movies. Actors start believing their own PR. It happens. He became a characterization of himself.

"It first started to get strange when we did a photo shoot with Japanese *Cosmopolitan*. Mickey wanted to art direct it himself and started putting his big fingers into the make-up and smearing it on the model that was in the shoot with him. As the Japanese people from the magazine watched, Mickey turned it into the darkest photo session ever. It was like a precursor to that movie he did, *Angel Heart*. He was pouring water on the model's head, pulling her hair back, ripping her blouse – all the Japanese stood up and turned their chairs to face the wall. It was, like, freakish.

"I left thinking, 'What did we just witness?' It was so weird. I thought, 'What's wrong with you, Mickey? You were so cute and so sweet.' He'd been such a nice guy, we would hang out and he even gave me three designer suits and a hat as presents.

"Mickey got really gross towards the mid-1990s. I'd run into him in places and he'd really say the foulest things. He really wasn't working then at all. He didn't look disfigured yet, just different. He was just nasty to people.

"I saw him in this restaurant on La Cienega Boulevard in LA...everyone was outside on the patio, he was sitting by the door with Carré Otis and he was just berating her in public and humiliating her and everyone was like 'Jeez, why doesn't he just shut up?' It went on and on. I didn't want to leave until they left in case he took a swing at me. We couldn't wait any longer so we left really quickly but he saw me and said, 'What about you, you cunt...aren't you going to say hello to me, you little cunt?' and I went, 'Mickey, just cool it.' It was like he just wanted to fight.

"When he switched careers to become a professional boxer,

I'm sure boxing was therapeutic for him. I just hope for Mickey that he doesn't go back to his arrogant ways. I'm happy that his acting career is going well again now but I didn't think he'd come back like this and win all those awards. *The Wrestler* is like his story but in the character of a wrestler. It's him. In the film, with all that long blond hair, he looks like a cross between Hulk Hogan's wife and the cowardly lion from *The Wizard of Oz*.

"As for his look off screen, he's now sort of grown into that face. It doesn't look as bad as it did eight years ago. If what happened to him happened to anyone else, they'd only be playing the Phantom of the Opera.

"He's an intriguing person to look at. But he now looks a little messy to me. I think he has extensions and he's probably still putting hair product in it. That look is great when it's your own hair. Mickey would look better if his hair was just slicked back, like Valentino. You don't want to see all that hair hanging. You're going to see that face with hair or no hair. But surrounding it with a mustache is a mistake, I'd get rid of that. It looks Asian, or like the boxer Manny Pacquiao. With make-up to make his face look moist, I'd make him as dreamy as possible.

"I think he's dressing wrong, too. There's too many little bits and pieces, like the shiny jewelry and that horrible chain around his waist. He needs to be a little bit cleaner. That look works on an eighteen-year-old skateboarder but for him there's too much going on. I wonder how Mickey feels now when he sees old pictures of himself like he used to look..."

Joe Wheeler, who still works as the doorman of Mickey's old apartment building, chuckles, "I'll never forget the time Mickey set his apartment on fire!" Mickey lived in Unit 11 on the ground floor of Granville Towers in LA from 1999 until 2003. Joe recalls, "One time, Mickey put a TV dinner in the oven to cook, went in the living room and fell asleep.

"I was working that night, looked over and saw all this smoke in the hallway. So another doorman and I rushed over, saw all the smoke was coming from Mickey's place, knocked loudly on his door, got him woken up and took care of it."

Joe adds: "Things were always happening to Mickey. One day we had to bandage him up after he got stabbed outside. He'd just gone out for a coffee and some guy attacked him on the street. The guy actually stabbed him and sliced Mickey's arm. Mickey got the guy off of him but came home and was bleeding. We have a first aid kit in the lobby and dealt with it. After that incident, we'd joke whenever he went outside, 'Do you need company today?'

"He felt comfortable and secure in his residence but I don't think he felt as comfortable out there in the world, it was just a feeling I got from him. He had a lot of trouble as far as the streets go because people looked at Mickey as the bad boy. People remembered his boxing career and thought they could take him. They would push him and try to goad him into a fight, like that guy with the knife.

"But Mickey was a quiet gentleman who stayed to himself mostly. The people that knew him liked him. Others that didn't were either scared of him or wanted to challenge him to something.

"My experience with him was nothing but pleasurable. He

was never rude or nasty to me and I never heard any complaints about him. None of the other doormen had anything bad to say about the man.

"He was down-to-earth. Granted, he had limousines picking him up here and taking him different places, but he wasn't ever like 'Hey, I'm Mickey Rourke!' Once he got to know you, Mickey was very magnificent. In fact, he once tried to get me a job working as his driver. It didn't come together but I was grateful to him.

"He was one of many big names we've had at the Granville. This building goes back to the 1930s and has always been associated with Hollywood people. Everyone from Greta Garbo to Paris Hilton has paid a visit at one time or another. Brendan Fraser from *The Mummy* movies lived in that same two-bedroom apartment as Mickey. He moved out of it and Mickey moved in – with his dogs.

"I remember he loved those dogs. He only had three with him when he was here. Beau Jack, Loki, and another Chihuahua. We have a dog run out the back and he would take them there. They never pooped in the lobby, Mickey wouldn't tolerate that – he wouldn't even tolerate poop in his own apartment. His home was very neat.

"But his clothes were very exotic. He dressed exactly the same ten years ago as he does now. You would never see him walking around in a T-shirt and shorts. It would always be an exotic combination of clothing. That was Mickey's style. He always dressed differently to other people whether he was going out for a coffee or going out for the evening.

"I saw a few of his friends here but mainly he would go out to them. He never brought too much home with him. He was single when he lived here but I think he was still very in love with his ex-wife Carré Otis, that's my personal opinion. I got that sense because of the things he talked about. When he brought her up there was a different tone in his voice. I took it as a respect and a love still held. He'd go out with somebody but he never had any other relationship here. He never brought the same girl back here twice unless it was a friend.

"I'd always thought Mickey had great acting ability and was aware of his earlier film work but I hadn't seen him do anything else in years. At times during those years at the Granville I got a sense he was down. I think it wore on him that he was just doing nothing. I don't think he liked doing nothing. Mickey seemed to like being an active person. But you can only be active if there's something to do.

"I am so ecstatically happy that Mickey Rourke is back working a lot now and is having all this success. I hope he makes millions and millions, I truly do. Given the right roles, I think he'll blossom into an actor just as good as De Niro or anyone else.

"I don't care what the world thinks about him, I think he's a great man. It's been my pleasure to know him. I'm thrilled he's back and wish him all the best."

When Mickey's friend Joe Rivera, one of America's leading fitness trainers, went to see *The Wrestler*, it was like a window into his pal's soul. He explains, "The heartbreak in the scene of him dancing in the bar with Marisa Tomei, well, that's Mickey. He's trying to be happy and all right but stuff is breaking up on the inside and that inner turmoil is surfacing a little. That's kind of what he's like in real life. Mickey's a sweetheart of a guy but also a tough cookie and a troubled soul. He really brought himself to that part.

"To be a good actor, you have to be in tune with your feelings, like he is, in order to find the truth of a scene. I know Mickey had a troubled past and had come from a rough background. I'd told him I was from East Harlem, which was tough, and he told me that Miami, where he was raised, wasn't that great either. It wasn't always like it is there now. You could tell from listening to him talk about it that he'd had a tough upbringing there. You knew this was a guy who'd experienced real danger, pain, and heartbreak.

"He did a really amazing job in *The Wrestler*, physically, emotionally, and performance-wise. I started out as an actor and one of my teachers back in New York would always say the best actor never gets caught acting and therefore the best actor ever was Lassie, because he was so real. In this movie, Mickey was Lassie.

"When I moved out to LA from New York, I never expected I was going to be rubbing elbows with people I grew up watching on screen and when you get to know them you never expect they are going to be regular cool people – but that was my experience with Mickey Rourke.

"I first met him in 1998 at Gold's Gym in Venice, LA, where he worked out next to me. That was great for me as I really respected him as an actor and especially admired the work he had done in *Body Heat*, *The Pope of Greenwich Village* and *Year of the Dragon*.

He was someone I aspired to be like."

As it turned out, muscle-bound Joe would become a superstar in the fitness world rather than in films and is now known as "the trainer to the trainer to the stars." He says, "It's funny where life takes you and it's funny that I would keep bumping into Mickey time and again over the years and we became friendly. Because I taught boxing and had fought some amateur fights, he connected with me over that and loved talking about boxing. For the first five years I knew him, every time I ran into him he'd say, 'Hey, Joe, you still boxing? I used to box but I can't anymore because the doctors told me if I get hit in the head, bad things are going to happen.' He would say the same thing every time. It was sweet.

"We used to run into each other at the same cool restaurants and clubs – and at one of those I realized Mickey was a true friend. At the end of the 1990s I was dating this model and her roommate was the most famous fitness model on the planet, a really nice looking girl but she wouldn't give me the time of day. I remember her trying to get into Atlantic, the hot place in LA at the time, when I was there with Mickey and she was outside in the line.

"The crowd at that place were like characters from that movie *Swingers*, a cool bunch of hipsters who, even if they came from Bumblefuck, Missouri, they'd adapted their personalities and would give you that New York vibe. If you were some fitness model from rural Texas dressed in a skimpy, tacky outfit, you'd look so out of place there that you were never getting in – no matter how good looking you were.

"But that night she suddenly saw me pop from behind the

velvet rope, shouted "Joe!" and started chatting me up. Suddenly, she was my best friend. She asked me to get her in, so I had a word with the bouncer and he let me in. Once she was inside, she went right back to not giving me the time of day...until she saw me standing at the bar drinking with Mickey Rourke!

"When I stepped away to go to the bathroom, she went straight over and tried to start up a conversation with Mickey, not knowing that I'd just been telling him what a user she was. So she says to him, 'You know Joe?' He says, 'Yeah, I know Joe,' and she goes, 'I know Joe, too!' So I get back and Mickey quietly tells me the girl is dropping my name to up her status and have conversations with the people in our group.

"Then we order a round of drinks and Mickey, in the style of his 'drinks for all my friends' character in *Barfly*, points out the fitness model to everyone, raises his glass, and toasts, 'To Joe's new best friend!'

"Surprisingly enough, she got the message and left immediately. But Mickey showed me in that moment what a good friend he was. Being a movie star, he could easily have slept with her – but instead he chose to hang out with friends. I thought it was so cool that he stuck up for me. Most guys in his situation wouldn't have done that. They'd have been like 'Who's Joe? Forget Joe...Joe Schmo. Hot girl, smoking body, half-naked already – let's go!'

"When you party with Mickey Rourke, it's fun and festive and there's no tension. He's warm hearted, matter of fact, down to earth, and kind of cool. But he can party hard. I gotta tell you, the boy can drink. He can definitely drink. If you're partying with Mickey, don't try to keep up with him, he'll hurt you. He likes his tequila but he can hold his liquor. I've seen him pounding shots but I've never seen him drunk or falling on his face like the rest of the people around us. There would always be lots of booze, a flock of people around him, hot girls everywhere. Things don't change. I was at the House of Blues in LA earlier this year and was told I'd just missed Mickey Rourke who had supposedly shown up with a bunch of Playboy Playmates.

"It's great that he's been welcomed back by Hollywood and I hope he keeps going on the path he's following now. If he'd won the Oscar this time it would have been the perfect *Cinderella* story but there's no reason why he can't be in that position again. He's always had the talent.

"Things weren't going so well for him a few years ago. He was apparently living beyond his means in that period. People who went to his home would say when you opened the refrigerator there was nothing in there – and it looked like he was going through a rough patch. But you didn't get that sense from Mickey himself. I've never noticed him being depressed. He's not the loud guy in the crew, he's more introspective and doesn't really talk about himself much.

"I gathered things weren't so good around six years ago when I was coming back to LA from a bachelor party in Las Vegas. My flight got delayed and I saw Mickey sitting on the floor with the hordes of other people who had been delayed on a Southwest Airlines flight. That's not the airline you fly when you have lots of money and there he was sitting with the masses waiting two hours to get on the plane. He looks over, smiles, and says, 'Hey, Joe! Are you still boxing? Because I used to box but I can't do it anymore…' So sweet!"

12
CHIC UNIQUE

When Mickey Rourke rocked up at Moscow's bleak Butyrka prison wearing blue designer moccasins with red tassels, it was clear that a true fashion individual had arrived at the grim building.

The fancy footwear he chose to wear in the stark surroundings where he was researching his Russian villain role in *Iron Man 2* was typical of his flair for out-of-place outfits. From the jails of Russia to the red carpets of Hollywood, Mickey can always be relied upon to wear something weird but somehow wonderful. Fashion is a passion and he has developed a style which is uniquely Mickey. Many may laugh at his madcap ensembles but Mickey is his own man and loves his flamboyant look.

And Mickey's awareness of controlling his image extends far beyond his choice of attire. Mickey now tucks his left hand into the waistband of his trousers whenever he's having his picture taken on a red carpet. It's a move which has become as much a signature pose for him as Victoria Beckham's "Posh" pout or Paris Hilton standing with one hand on her hip.

When he started doing it at the January 2009 awards shows, it just looked weird and maybe more suited to a rock star, but since then the confident, casual gesture has become an accepted part of the whole eccentric Mickey Rourke look. After all these years of being photographed, he knows his best angle and the hand down the pants is the familiar pose he strikes when ready to show off his latest fashion ensemble to the best effect.

* * *

This strutting peacock of a star certainly makes the most of a variety of fashion trademarks, including the ever present chain, big open-neck shirts, unbuttoned cuffs, crazy jackets, feminine scarves, shiny suits, tinted shades, and fancy shoes.

While most men have only a few pairs of shoes, and usually in only black or brown, Mickey is the male version of Imelda Marcos and has countless colorful pairs, including some especially striking ones in metallic orange, shiny gold-and-silver trainers, and a pair of burgundy velvet slippers. His favorite shoe designers are Jean-Michel Cazabat and Roberto Cavalli.

When one of his hugely overweight suitcases was examined at London's Heathrow Airport in February 2009, it was found to be full of nothing but shoes. Officials first thought he must have put his heavy British Academy Award in there, as he was on his way back to the States after the BAFTA award ceremony, but, instead, the 36-kg weight was caused by the forty pairs of shoes he had packed for his eight-day trip. Mickey was made to redistribute his footwear among other cases before he was cleared for travel.

He wears plenty of bling on his fingers – sometimes sporting four rings at a time – and even has some in his mouth, courtesy of a tooth capped in gold.

Mickey wears sunglasses and tinted spectacles everywhere,

but that may have less to do with fashion choice and more to do with him having conjunctivitis. He got the condition, also known as pink-eye, from all the Vaseline and leather gloves slamming into his eyes during the boxing years and it tends to reappear when he gets his make-up done for movies. He is often seen sporting Sama's Press sunglasses but also likes Loree Rodkin and classic Ray-Ban Wayfarers.

Mickey's outfits may look like a haphazard series of unfortunate events, strange choices put together off the cuff, just like his award acceptance speeches, but a lot of thought goes into each ensemble. Even more thought since he started employing a stylist. Michael Fisher was hired by Fox Searchlight to style Mickey during *The Wrestler*'s attention-grabbing press and publicity tour, but then remained with the star during awards season and beyond. Once Mickey realized Michael was willing to help him express his own style, rather than impose radically different ideas, a thriving professional relationship was born.

Fisher, who has worked as an assistant to ace photographer Annie Leibovitz and leading stylist Rachel Zoe and provided fashion tips to the likes of Beyoncé Knowles and Kate Hudson, tweaked his client's look with additions and ideas, while still keeping it innately Mickey. They both wanted the clothes Mickey wore to be as dramatic and memorable as his performance in *The Wrestler*. The first thing Mickey said to him was, "I'm not George Clooney and I'm never going to be George Clooney," a reference to Clooney's priding himself on having worn the same Calvin Klein tuxedo to Hollywood events for years.

The play safe option of smart black suit with a white shirt as favored by Clooney and countless other actors was never going to be for him. Mickey takes risks in his fashion choices just as he does in his roles. That strategy paid off, with rebel Mickey's red carpet selections getting as much if not more attention than anything worn by actresses during the 2009 awards season. His butch, bizarre, but brilliant outfits brought a kind of disheveled elegance to showbiz events that made Mickey the talk of the fashion world as well as the film community. His dashing new look was variously described as "Miami dandy," "Modern Musketeer," "Salvador Dali creepy," "wacky and tacky," "Toad of Toad Hall," and "stolen from a Cirque du Soleil performer." Crueler critics suggested the clothes were just a deliberate attempt to distract from whatever he had done to his face.

He may have been flying by the seat of his Dolce & Gabbana pants during the whole process, but he was definitely being noticed and, with the stylist's assistance, Mickey's look clearly went from a bit of a mess to kind of cool. As the awards season events turned into an endless parade of trophies for *Slumdog Millionaire* and Kate Winslet, the only tantalizing suspense came from the question: what will Mickey Rourke wear next?

Mickey tended to stick to his favorite European designers, wearing Dolce to the BAFTAs and Screen Actors Guild awards, Billionaire Couture (owned by Formula One mogul Flavio Briatore) to the Golden Globes, Jean-Paul Gaultier to the Paris premiere of *The Wrestler,* and Gaultier again at the Oscars. He teamed all these stylish designer clothes of gold, silver, midnight blue, and other striking colors with his macho outlaw accessories and somehow pulled it off. Nobody else could wear such a sartorial riot of different outfits and get away with them but Mickey managed it, and became an unlikely trendsetter in the process. At the 2009 Oscars, he was the unanimous pick of fashion experts as best-dressed man thanks to his ivory Gaultier tuxedo accessorized with the pendant honoring his late dog, Loki.

Stylish rebel Mickey was so embraced by the fashion community that he landed a front-row seat at the 2009 New York Fashion Week show of designer Domenico Vacca, an Italian ex-lawyer-turned-red-hot designer. Mickey sat next to Forest Whitaker who wore the designer's clothes when he picked up his Best Actor Oscar for *The Last King of Scotland*.

Mickey was back on the awards circuit in 2010, usually presenting the best actress awards, and brought his maverick fashion sense with him. His two most memorable outfits were his BAFTA Awards selection – a shiny gray suit with a vest underneath but no shirt...oh, and his hair in a top-knot – and his Golden Globes choice – a punk rock cowboy tuxedo based on his own design and made for him by Sylvester Stallone's tailor, David August. At the *Iron Man 2* Hollywood premiere he wore another David August outfit, a three-piece brown suit with what looked like crocodile print on the lapels. But animal lover Mickey was keen to stress to reporters on the red carpet that the animal skin wasn't real and no creatures had been harmed in the making of his outfit.

Mickey likes high-end clothes stores the way gamblers like betting shops and, during his many trips to London, has been a frequent visitor to the Harrods menswear department and the tailors of Savile Row. But he likes Italian designers best for the macho aesthetic they bring to their clothes.

Adding to the macho look are the seven tattoos Mickey has on his body, which include an American-Indian symbol for strength, an Oriental symbol for "soul and spirit," a leopard's head with the Chinese ideogram for *Year of the Dragon,* and also the words "Carré Forever."

Mickey attributes his lifelong interest in fashion to both his late grandmother, who was always a sharp dresser, and his background in Miami, a trendsetting city where flamboyant styles were commonplace. After leaving school, he did toy with the idea of studying either fashion or interior design but his poor academic results made a college place unlikely and he instead hung out with his friends and dressed in as cool a way as he could. His pride and joy back then was a pair of handmade platform shoes in black and pink. Mickey stands just under 6 ft tall but in those crazy things he looked 6 ft-5 in.

Around 1973, his absolute fashion icon was David Bowie and Mickey would dress like the glam-rock hero in stack-heeled boots, tight leather trousers, and cut-off shirts. The Ziggy Stardust wannabe even had green hair at one point. When the pair became friends years later, the pop star was thrilled to hear he had been such an influence on Mickey's life.

Mickey loved David's music as well as his outfits. Bowie thought his friend had some musical skills of his own and even let him perform on one of his records. Mickey can be heard performing a rap duet with David in the track "Shining Star (Makin' My Love)" on the 1987 Bowie album *Never Let Me*

Down.

Around that time, Mickey had developed a particular look of his own which made him a style icon around the world – the black sunglasses, the cigarette drooping from his lips, the unkempt hair, the stubble, stylish jackets, and black T-shirts – it was all about attitude and cool. Things fell apart a little in the boxing years: the endless hoodies and gym pants he wore back then were far from glamorous. But then his mind was clearly much more on fights than fashion.

In the wilderness years, post-boxing and pre-comeback, he spent much of his time pumping iron and hanging out with bodybuilders at Gold's Gym in Venice, California, and his sweat-soaked fashions of the time reflected the company he was keeping rather than the movie star he aspired to become again. He looked more likely to rob a liquor store than steal scenes in a major movie. Little wonder that agent David Unger ordered him to lose the gym clothes and smarten up as part of the career comeback strategy for his client.

He has tried out various looks in the last two decades – we've had hip-hop Mickey, biker Mickey, and foppish Mickey among others. Rourke has worn all manner of eye-catching outfits, from silk paisley shirts to gold pin-striped suits. Through it all, he has stuck to two key rules – he never wears red and hardly ever wears underwear.

This mix of flamboyant but quality clothes and tough guy accessories he goes for now is an undoubtedly stylish combination. Darren Aronofsky has a theory that Mickey wears all these eye-catching outfits as a defense mechanism to stop people looking into his eyes – the windows to the soul. He has certainly hidden behind a mask or his characters in the past, but these days Mickey seems a whole lot happier and is just being himself – and looking good doing it.

Long may he continue to work the red carpet with panache, keep taking fashion chances, and get everyone talking with his decadent selections. It may not be to everyone's taste, but the man's certainly got style.

13
FAR FROM EXPENDABLE

Mickey Rourke felt on top of the world when he was offered the main villain's role in *Iron Man 2* – until he saw how much he would be paid for the follow-up to a film which made half a billion dollars worldwide. The offer was $250,000, a princely sum to most of us but an insultingly low one for an Oscar-nominated actor in a big-budget blockbuster.

Now Mickey had a dilemma. After *The Wrestler* had made him successful again, but not wealthy, he had resolved to chase the best roles rather than the best pay checks, and he was extremely keen to act alongside Robert Downey Jr. in the sequel to one of Hollywood's best recent hits. But even so, could he really let moneybags Marvel Entertainment get him on the cheap? They had already shown they wouldn't be held to ransom on this project by replacing Terrence Howard with Don Cheadle after Howard protested his pay deal for returning as the superhero's sidekick, Lt. Col. James Rhodes.

Talks continued for weeks as Marvel claimed money problems. But when its latest report showed huge fourth-quarter profits of $63 million, mostly due to DVD sales of the first *Iron Man* film, it was hard to keep making that argument. In the end, it took the personal intervention of Robert Downey Jr. to persuade movie bosses to fork out more for Mickey. Like Mickey, Downey was a troubled but talented actor who had made a cool comeback and he knew the sequel would be a whole lot more special with Mickey in it. The deal was finally done in March 2009 – a month ahead of filming – with the increase in pay undisclosed but said to be substantial.

Then in-demand Mickey got another amazing offer – to join the all-star cast of Sylvester Stallone's rip-roaring action movie, *The Expendables*. Remembering how Sly had stuck by him in the lean years, he eagerly accepted the chance to work with him again and add his name to the film's eye-catching cast of 1980s icons, which along with Rourke and Stallone also included Arnold Schwarzenegger and Bruce Willis. *The Expendables* was to be released in August 2010, just three months after *Iron Man 2*, thereby putting Rourke right at the center of two big budget summer blockbusters.

After years in little independent films that hardly anyone saw, Mickey was now in the movies that mattered. Furthermore, at an age when other famous actors reluctantly get pushed towards the Hollywood retirement home, comeback king Mickey was proving himself to be far from expendable.

* * *

Men-on-a-mission movie *The Expendables* is about a crack team of hired guns sent to a South American country to overthrow the ruthless dictator in charge. As the mission begins, the mercenaries discover that the situation is not what it appears, and the band of brothers is soon battling deceit and betrayal.

Writer-director and star Sylvester Stallone assembled a troop of tough guy legends to appear alongside him – martial arts maestro Jet Li, *The Transporter*'s Jason Statham, wrestling great Stone Cold Steve Austin, Ultimate Fighting Championship star Randy Couture, ex-NFL linebacker Terry Crews, Sly's *Rocky IV* co-star Dolph Lundgren, and screen veteran Eric Roberts. Stallone offered roles to fellow action icons Jean-Claude Van Damme and Steven Seagal, but both men turned down the chance to join the party.

Mickey had no hesitation in signing on to star as Tool, an arms dealer and tattoo artist who provides the mercenaries with their firepower. He wore his own clothes in the film and had a great time on set. Going to work with a mixture of real life fighters and old friends, all of whom respected him, was most definitely his idea of fun.

Despite all the hard-man roles he has played over the years, Rourke hasn't killed that many people on screen – at least not compared with some of his co-stars in *The Expendables*. Mickey's characters have a total of 54 screen kills, which compares unfavorably to Jason Statham's 137, Bruce Willis's 187, and Jet Li's 209, while his figure is positively dwarfed by Sylvester Stallone's 338 and Arnold Schwarzenegger's 510.

It was a huge casting coup for Sly Stallone to get both Arnold Schwarzenegger and Bruce Willis on board for cameo roles in his orgy of action – especially because Willis was in the middle of shooting another movie at the time, the comedy *Cop Out*, and the Governator was busy running California. Each time a filming date was agreed, it kept changing because Arnie suddenly had a budget crisis or a fire to deal with. But eventually, at 8:10 A.M. on 25 October 2009, cameras rolled at the Hollywood Presbyterian Church on a scene which marked the first time the tough guy trio of Sly, Arnie, and Bruce ever appeared on screen together. Bruce plays a shady mogul who hires Sly's team for the mission on the recommendation of a fellow soldier of fortune played by Arnie.

By that time, most of the movie, shot on location in Louisiana and Brazil, was in the can. Public anticipation was already building for this greatest ever gathering of action heroes in one film. When the first trailer was released on You Tube, it got a million views in its first week. With all that testosterone among the big names on set, there was no holding back from the macho movie actors in the close combat scenes. It was such a tough shoot that Stallone suffered a hairline fracture of his neck while filming a fight scene with Steve Austin and had to have emergency surgery that left him with a metal plate inserted in his neck. Mickey, who came into the film nursing that injury suffered when arm wrestling a rugby player in a London pub, escaped the rough shoot unscathed. That was a relief because the work offers kept on coming and the roles were stacking up.

Next he shot a dramatic, romantic, and very different lead role in *Passion Play*, as a down-on-his-luck 1950s trumpet player named Nate who comes to the rescue of a caged circus freak with angel-like wings, played by *Transformers* sexpot Megan Fox. His co-star has often come in for criticism that her looks are a lot more impressive than her talent, but Rourke thinks she's had a raw deal and after working with Megan calls her the best young actress he has ever starred with. The intriguing film reunites

Rourke with his *Desperate Hours* leading lady Kelly Lynch, who plays his bartender best friend, and also features Bill Murray.

Busy Mickey followed that one with *Immortals*, a Clash of the Titans – type mythological adventure movie in which a young Greek warrior battles the ancient Gods in a bid to save mankind. Rourke plays evil King Hyperion and his co-stars include John Hurt as Old Zeus and *Slumdog Millionaire*'s Freida Pinto as a princess. Visual flair is the signature of director Tarsem Singh and his style, along with Rourke's talent, should set this one apart from other sword and sandals pics.

Already completed and awaiting release is *13*, a crime thriller that Mickey calls a "wonderful" film. He plays anti-hero Jesse James Jefferson, a tobacco-chewing Texas cowboy and ex-convict who becomes embroiled in a version of Russian roulette where high rollers bet on the lives of kidnapped outsiders. Jason Statham, Ray Winstone, Ray Liotta, and 50 Cent make up an impressive ensemble cast. Also in the film is one of Mickey's oldest and dearest friends, larger-than-life Hell's Angel-turned-bodyguard-turned-actor and DJ Chuck Zito, who appears as one of the gang who kidnaps Jefferson so he can be a player in the deadly game.

Mickey has recently been in talks about starring as a grizzled biker in a film called *Hell's Angels*, inspired by the history of the famous motorcycle gang, to be directed by old friend and colleague Tony Scott, for whom he may also star in a crime drama named *Potsdamer Platz* about a New Jersey gangster family looking to expand its empire internationally. Other projects he has been circling include *Broken Horses*, a Bollywood-meets-Hollywood gangster drama, and the biopic *Genghis Khan,* in which Mickey would play the Mongolian warrior. And he hopes to one day film *Wild Horses,* which has taken him the past eighteen years to write, about two long estranged brothers taking a motor biking trip together.

There are no comedies among his upcoming pictures. In fact, he hasn't fronted any comedy films in his entire career, because that's something he's had no desire to tackle. But dramas are a different matter and, striking while the iron's hot, he's got them stacked up one after another.

So Mickey is busier than ever, back in the big time, and aiming to stay there. Now that he's finally showing signs of understanding how show business works, Rourke, together with his agent, is putting together a plan to keep his career hot and become a respected elder statesman of Hollywood. The idea is that he will carry on his much improved work ethic by being consistent in his performances and professionalism, select only movies with integrity, work only with directors he respects and co-stars he likes, and not shoot his mouth off so much. If he can achieve all that, then Mickey should remain a major figure in movies for a long time.

Success like that would represent one of the most remarkable career turnarounds in Tinseltown history. Mickey Rourke looks like he has gone twelve rounds with a heavyweight champion and maybe several more with a cosmetic surgeon...but he's still in there punching. Traditional wisdom would seem to be against him following up *The Wrestler* and *Iron Man 2* with more awards and hit films. After all, there are few lead roles for actors over fifty and Mickey threw away many chances at lasting stardom. But he's also shown it's always wrong to count him out.

In his favor is the fact that Mickey occupies a unique place in the film business as just about the only star around right now that can convincingly play the vulnerable tough guy. He has the same tough-on-the-outside, tender-on-the-inside quality that characterized Hollywood legends Marlon Brando, Clark Gable, and Humphrey Bogart.

After years of being a punch line, praise is now coming his way and Mickey has made time in his packed schedule to accept the accolades. He made an emotional visit in June 2009 to the place that helped make him the great actor he is today – the Actors' Studio. He went back to be interviewed about his career for an episode of acclaimed cable TV series *Inside The Actors' Studio,* and was touched by the warm reception from current students who hung on his every word. He took time afterwards to shake plenty of hands and talk to the audience, humbly accepting congratulations on his comeback and best wishes for the many movies ahead of him.

That same month, he was the toast of Spike TV's Guy Awards where his victory as Guy of the Year was loudly celebrated by a host of fellow stars including Quentin Tarantino, Brad Pitt, Ben Stiller, Halle Berry, and Clint Eastwood. Sacha Baron Cohen was there also, appearing as his camp character Bruno to pay an amusing tribute by cheekily joking, "Mickey Rourke was so sexy in *The Wrestler* as a broken-down piece of meat – which is, coincidentally, what I had in my hand at the end of that movie."

Mickey no longer looked out of place in such A-list company.

After years of struggle to get back to this point, he was a genuine movie star once again. Clearly, the days of waiting for the phone to ring with film offers are long gone. Thanks to behaving himself, thanks to therapy, and especially thanks to *The Wrestler*, he has the chance to work on a string of hugely promising projects.

Now that his career is no longer a train wreck, the task is to make the most of this long-awaited opportunity. He is determined not to mess it up. Mickey says, "I was out of the game so many years and didn't realize it would take this long to get back. But there ain't no quit in me and I'm grateful to have this chance now. I appreciate it a lot that people trust me again after me raising hell for years. But I know this is my last chance. I'm not going to have another one. I'll always have that little man inside me with two axes but I've got to learn to keep him the fuck quiet."

But you can banish any thoughts that this more serious and mild-mannered Mickey is dispensing with his dangerous and eccentric sides. A look around the contents of his New York home will confirm that. Mickey is now back living in Greenwich Village, and journalist Steve Garbarino visited the star's rented townhouse as part of an excellent profile of the actor for *Maxim* magazine. He found it to be a place of fascinating contrasts. As well as ornate chandeliers, a marble fireplace, and fancy furniture, the home contains a loaded handgun, a stripper's pole, and a rubber dildo suction-cupped to a wall. There's also a punching bag, portraits of Loki, Carré Otis, and Richard Harris, and plenty of prescription pills.

Mickey regularly invites friends round for Mexican nights where they eat take-out tacos and burritos washed down with

Corona beer. When he fancies something grander, celebrity-packed restaurant The Waverly Inn is just two streets away.

During all the years he lived in Los Angeles, Mickey never knew his neighbors, but now he is seemingly on first-name terms with everyone in the neighborhood. Happy in his home life and content in his career, it's a triumphant turnaround in fortunes for the film star.

Many movie fans had watched in dismay as Mickey's promising career imploded, and his riches to rags story can be seen as a cautionary tale for up-and-coming actors. He dropped so far and so fast that his life could have been a blues song. But the way he turned things around can only be admired. His posse pushed off and his wives walked out but Mickey's talent never left him. That was clear from his acting in *The Wrestler*, a piece of work that revived memories of other spellbinding performances for which Mickey Rourke deserves a place among the acting greats.

He could get one, too, if an ongoing campaign by fans to get Mickey his own star on the Hollywood Walk of Fame proves successful. The Oscar nominee certainly seems more deserving than several of the actors selected for that particular honor in 2010, such as Jon Cryer, Sam Waterston, and Mark Wahlberg. And those loyal Mickey Rourke fans are suddenly everywhere now – from Facebook to MySpace – and spreading the word on lovingly maintained websites like UniquelyRourke.com.

After some lonely years, Mickey has more friends in his life now, and ones who are a positive influence. Among them is fellow Oscar-nominee Brad Pitt, who shares Mickey's enthusiasm for motorbikes. Mickey can't afford to buy the really expensive models Brad owns, but enjoys chatting about bikes with the heart-throb superstar.

Mickey's wild, high-octane life appears to be calming down at last and heading in the right direction. He is still in therapy, although his appointments are now down to a couple of phone calls per week. He is still in regular contact with Father Peter Colapietro and always has Christmas dinner with him at the church rectory. And Mickey continues to pray – no longer for himself, but now for the safety of his dogs, which he has lately been missing terribly while away so often filming.

Mickey is still wrestling with his demons, but it's a fight he seems to be winning. Randy "The Ram" Robinson couldn't give himself a future in *The Wrestler,* but it certainly looks as if the movie has given Mickey a very bright one indeed.

Mickey Rourke Filmography

FILM ROLES

1941 (1979)
Role: Private Reese
Director: Steven Spielberg
Co-star: John Belushi

Fade to Black (1980)
Role: Richie
Director: Vernon Zimmerman
Co-star: Denis Christopher

Heaven's Gate (1980)
Role: Nick Ray
Director: Michael Cimino
Co-star: Kris Kristofferson

Body Heat (1981)
Role: Teddy Lewis
Director: Lawrence Kasdan
Co-star: William Hurt

Diner (1982)
Role: Robert "Boogie" Sheftell

Director: Barry Levinson
Co-star: Steve Guttenberg

Eureka (1983)
Role: Aurelio D'Amato
Director: Nicolas Roeg
Co-star: Gene Hackman

Rumble Fish (1983)
Role: Motorcycle Boy
Director: Francis Ford Coppola
Co-star: Matt Dillon

The Pope of Greenwich Village (1984)
Role: Charlie Moran
Director: Stuart Rosenberg
Co-star: Eric Roberts

Year of the Dragon (1985)
Role: Captain Stanley White
Director: Michael Cimino
Co-star: John Lone

9½ Weeks (1986)
Role: John Gray
Director: Adrian Lyne
Co-star: Kim Basinger

Angel Heart (1987)
Role: Harry Angel
Director: Alan Parker
Co-star: Robert De Niro

Barfly (1987)
Role: Henry Chinaski
Director: Barbet Schroeder
Co-star: Faye Dunaway

A Prayer for the Dying (1987)
Role: Martin Fallon
Director: Mike Hodges
Co-star: Bob Hoskins

Homeboy (1988)
Role: Johnny Walker
Director: Michael Seresin
Co-star: Christopher Walken

Francesco (1989)
Role: Francesco, aka Francis of Assisi
Director: Liliana Cavani
Co-star: Helena Bonham Carter

Johnny Handsome (1989)
Role: John Sedley, aka Johnny Mitchell
Director: Walter Hill
Co-star: Morgan Freeman

Wild Orchid (1989)

Role: James Wheeler
Director: Zalman King
Co-star: Carré Otis

Desperate Hours (1990)

Role: Michael Bosworth
Director: Michael Cimino
Co-star: Anthony Hopkins

Harley Davidson and the Marlboro Man (1991)

Role: Harley
Director: Simon Wincer
Co-star: Don Johnson

White Sands (1992)

Role: Gorman Lennox
Director: Roger Donaldson
Co-star: Willem Dafoe

F.T.W. (1993)

Role: Frank T. Wells
Director: Michael Karbelnikoff
Co-star: Lori Singer

Fall Time (1995)

Role: Florence
Director: Paul Warner
Co-star: Stephen Baldwin

Exit in Red (1996)

Role:	Ed Altman
Director:	Yurek Bogayevicz
Co-star:	Anthony Michael Hall

Bullet (1996)

Role:	Butch "Bullet" Stein
Director:	Julien Temple
Co-star:	Tupac Shakur

Double Team (1997)

Role:	Stavros
Director:	Tsui Hark
Co-star:	Jean-Claude Van Damme

Another 9½ Weeks (1997)

Role:	John Gray
Director:	Anne Goursaud
Co-star:	Angie Everhart

The Rainmaker (1997)

Role:	Bruiser Stone
Director:	Francis Ford Coppola
Co-star:	Matt Damon

Buffalo '66 (1998)

Role:	The Bookie
Director:	Vincent Gallo
Co-star:	Vincent Gallo

Point Blank (1998)
Role: Rudy Ray
Director: Max Earl Beesley
Co-star: Danny Trejo

Thursday (1998)
Role: Kasarov
Director: Skip Woods
Co-star: Thomas Jane

Cousin Joey (1999)
Role: Brother
Director: Sante D'Orazio
Co-star: Jaye Davidson

Shergar (1999)
Role: Gavin O'Rourke
Director: Dennis Lewiston
Co-star: Ian Holm

Out in Fifty (1999)
Role: Jack Bracken
Director: Bojesse Christopher
Co-star: Christina Applegate

Shades (1999)
Role: Paul S. Sullivan
Director: Eric Van Looy
Co-star: Gene Bervoets

Animal Factory (2000)

Role: Jan the Actress

Director: Steve Buscemi

Co-star: Edward Furlong

Get Carter (2000)

Role: Cyrus Paice

Director: Stephen Kay

Co-star: Sylvester Stallone

The Pledge (2001)

Role: James Olstad

Director: Sean Penn

Co-star: Jack Nicholson

They Crawl (2001)

Role: Tiny Frakes

Director: John Allardice

Co-star: Tamara Davies

Picture Claire (2001)

Role: Eddie

Director: Bruce McDonald

Co-star: Juliette Lewis

Spun (2002)

Role: The Cook

Director: Jonas Åkerlund

Co-star: Jason Schwartzman

Masked and Anonymous (2003)

Role: Edmund

Director: Larry Charles

Co-star: Bob Dylan

Once Upon a Time in Mexico (2003)

Role: Billy Chambers

Director: Robert Rodriguez

Co-star: Antonio Banderas

Man on Fire (2004)

Role: Jordan Kalfus

Director: Tony Scott

Co-star: Denzel Washington

Sin City (2005)

Role: Marv

Director: Robert Rodriguez

Co-star: Jessica Alba

Domino (2005)

Role: Ed Moseby

Director: Tony Scott

Co-star: Keira Knightley

Stormbreaker (2006)

Role: Darrius Sayle

Director: Geoffrey Sax

Co-star: Alex Pettyfer

The Wrestler (2008)

Role: Randy "The Ram" Robinson
Director: Darren Aronofsky
Co-star: Marisa Tomei

Killshot (2009)

Role: Armand "The Blackbird" Degas
Director: John Madden
Co-star: Diane Lane

The Informers (2009)

Role: Peter
Director: Gregor Jordan
Co-star: Kim Basinger

Iron Man 2 (2010)

Role: Ivan/Whiplash
Director: Jon Favreau
Co-star: Robert Downey Jr.

The Expendables (2010)

Role: Tool
Director: Sylvester Stallone
Co-star: Sylvester Stallone

TELEVISION ROLES

WrestleMania XXV (2009)
Role: Himself

Thicker Than Blood (1998)
Role: Father Frank Larkin

The Last Outlaw (1993)
Role: Graff

Hardcase (1981)
Role: Perk Dawson

Rape and Marriage: The Rideout Case (1980)
Role: John Rideout

Act of Love (1980)
Role: Joseph Cybulkowski

City in Fear (1980)
Role: Tony Pate

SCREENPLAYS
(as "Sir" Eddie Cook)

Bullet (1996)

F.T.W. (1994)
Homeboy (1988)

MAJOR AWARDS

Golden Globe – Best Actor (Drama) – *The Wrestler*
BAFTA Film Award – Best Actor – *The Wrestler*
Independent Spirit Award – Best Actor – *The Wrestler*
Saturn Award – Best Supporting Actor – *Sin City*
National Society of Film Critics – Best Supporting Actor – *Diner*
Academy Award Nomination for Best Actor – *The Wrestler*

VIDEO GAME VOICEOVERS

Rogue Warrior: Black Razor (2009)
Role: Richard "Demo Dick" Marcinko

True Crime: New York City (2005)
Role: Terry Higgins

Driv3r (2004)
Role: Jericho

JAPANESE TV COMMERCIALS

Suntory, Lark and Daihatsu

POP VIDEO APPEARANCES

John Rich ("Shuttin' Detroit Down") 2009
Enrique Iglesias ("Hero") 2001

MUSIC

Music supervisor on the 1996 film *Bullet*
Provided the mid-song rap on the David Bowie song "Shining Star (Makin' My Love)" which was on the 1987 Bowie album *Never Let Me Down*.

About the Author

Based in Beverly Hills, British-born journalist Alessandro "Sandro" Monetti is one of the world's most experienced and respected show business writers. He has covered the Hollywood scene for over twenty years making frequent TV appearances as a showbiz expert and giving Masters-level university lectures on how to interview celebrities. Monetti has worked as a media consultant for *Sky TV*, as showbiz correspondent for *News of the World*, and as a columnist for *Smash Hits* magazine. He now writes entertainment features for the *Sunday Express* and a gossip column for the *Daily Star Sunday* newspapers. Monetti provides celebrity reports for BBC radio stations and moderates Q&As with the stars at BAFTA's LA movie screenings. He has closely followed Mickey Rourke's roller-coaster career as both reporter and fan for the past 20 years.